For Jenny

*Your strength inspires me*

# A DIFFERENT KIND OF EDGE

Transitioning from Skater to Coach:

A Guide to Figure Skating Foundations

JESSICA RENSCH

First paperback edition December 2022

*Edited by Jolyn Hecht*

ISBN 9798369708422 (paperback)
www.jessicarensch.com

# A DIFFERENT KIND OF EDGE

Transitioning from Skater to Coach:  A Guide to Figure Skating Foundations

# CHAPTER I

## IT'S ALL CONNECTED

I remember feeling lost and confused in my early coaching years. I knew how to skate. I was a good skater. Anything I taught was something I could execute very well on the ice. Yet somehow, I felt stuck and unable to teach skating well.

As a perfectionist, I would ask myself how it could be so difficult to teach something that I was good at doing. But that was exactly the issue. I skate by feeling – as so many other skaters who begin at a young age do. I could hold an outside edge and it felt natural, and I didn't have to think about it. Therefore, I had no idea how to describe the details that go into holding an edge. It's like trying to explain how to pick an object up and hold it in our hands. We do it without thinking about it and we often don't know how to break the process down and explain it.

In those early days of coaching, I searched everywhere for a book that carefully explained the techniques behind skating. It was hard for me to remember the basics. I wanted to be more specific about where a skater should press on the blade at certain times, how to teach jump rotation, increase speed, etc. I could visualize my early lessons and I could feel my coach's instruction on arm placement and holds– but the actual language of the basics escaped me. I struggled to find the answers and pride and embarrassment often stopped me from asking other coaches for guidance.

After years of research, training, getting the nerve to ask advice from other coaches, and slowly working through elements to find my own techniques, I decided to write a book to share with other professional coaches and skaters based on what I have learned. This is the book I wanted but couldn't find when I started my coaching career. This book is a resource for the skater who wants to transition from being an athlete to being a coach. I hope it can inspire you to not only build a strong baseline, but help you create your own ideas about coaching. The most amazing thing I found during my coaching journey is how everything in figure skating connects and builds on itself.

Figure skating is both an art and a science. Webster's Dictionary defines art as something that is created with imagination and skill and that is beautiful or that expresses important ideas or feelings. Skating is both imaginative and depicts beauty and emotional expression. For example, skaters and coaches can take a technical element like a swing roll or a three-turn and add artistic arms and facial expressions to match the music and turn the element into something moving that touches the hearts of the audience. That is why people all over the world tune in to watch skating competitions or travel to see skating shows; the technique is impressive as skaters perform things that once were considered impossible, and the performance connects skaters to the audience. It's moving, inspiring, and uplifting.

However, it is also a science. Webster's dictionary defines science as knowledge about or study of the natural world based on facts learned through experiments and observation. If you watch skaters from 50 years ago, it's apparent that the nature of skating has transformed through coaches' usage of observation and experimentation and the actual scientific study of figure skating with relation to kinesiology, brain development, physics, etc. Figure skaters retrain their brains to train their bodies to spin quickly, lean deeply on edges, and jump quickly and land correctly. Through the study of physics, coaches can confirm quicker skill mastery. Because of this experimentation, skaters have pushed past what once were seen as limits and have been able to magnify jump height, increase spin positioning and speed, and even change the structure of blades and boots to better support skating as well.

How incredible is it that figure skating coaches get to be both scientists and artists while coaching a sport? This duo allows for creativity within proven scientific measures. Therefore, if you train yourself on the finite details involved in the sport, you can create big picture changes and beautiful programs and patterns on the ice.

*Who am I?*

You might wonder who I am and why you should believe a word I have to say about figure skating. I am a coach who is passionate about figure skating and fascinated by how it works. The point of this book is not to agree with my every thought or technique; it is to help you question and explore your own coaching philosophy and build a strong coaching foundation. In fact, I encourage you to question things throughout your coaching career so that you can land on the best possible solutions for yourself as a coach. Some of the things that work for me may not work for you, but I believe the best way to continue to grow as coaches is to share our findings, remain open-minded, and develop a unique coaching plan that works for each of us as individuals as we learn from one another.

I have spent countless hours in conferences, researching online, shadowing lessons of more seasoned coaches, taking diligent notes, and discovering new things through trial and error on the ice. I feel a responsibility to give back and share what I have found with the greater figure skating community. It is my hope to reach as many coaches and skaters as possible who may feel lost like I did when I first started coaching. Even those who are confident in their techniques, can always benefit from hearing different perspectives to keep the sport interesting.

*My Teacher Life*

I was once an elementary school teacher. My students' classroom experience was strengthened by the way I taught each unique person based on their individual learning styles, in a group. That carried over into beginner group lessons in figure skating. The same creative ways I kept students on track in the classroom benefitted me on the ice.

I also learned through classroom experience how important parent communication was for the whole team (student, teacher/coach, and parent). I have experience working with large groups of children and finding ways to teach each unique person based on their individual learning styles. I have learned how to manage large groups, find creative ways to keep everyone on track, and I have a lot of experience with parent communication and group management.

*My Skating Director Life*

I was an interim skating director in a first-generation ice town. This meant I spent a good portion of my time providing basic education to the public.

My daily tasks included resolving coach conflicts, handling unexpected situations such as injuries, making difficult leadership decisions, and constantly searching for new solutions to the many problems that arise when managing a skating community. I learned that a plan for the day was more of a guideline. For example, just as I would sit down to work on the Learn-to-Skate schedule, a member from the club would barge into the office to lecture me on not canceling enough freestyles for their club event. Or a group lesson parent would call to lecture me on how another coach is running their class. My diplomacy skills were often tested as I tried my best to graciously listen to parents *and* support the coach while also sharing parent feedback with coaches so that we could continuously progress as a staff.

I quickly discovered that people love to look at decisions in terms of how they are personally affected while failing to look at the bigger picture for the program. The skating director's job is to make choices for the good of the community and often the reactions from others who are selfishly thinking about their needs can be taxing. The difficult decisions and conversations taught me a lot about leadership and figure skating. I also learned how to accept the fact that you can't please everyone. That's a difficult concept for many.

*My Coach Life*

Coaching is one of my favorite pastimes. It's a difficult and challenging career, but I love it. I enjoy connecting with other skaters and supporting them in their goals. The bond that forms between coaches and skaters is special and it's so much fun to see how every lesson with each skater is different, based on their personalities. The best part is watching them progress over time.

However, not all aspects of coaching are easy. There are times when my decisions are questioned. Parents have sent me long and angry emails after their child did not place well in a competition or pass a test. Clearly, those parents fail to take responsibility for their actions like getting their child to the rink to practice, and their skater's actions (practicing with intention) when they choose to place 100% of the blame on a coach. This type of parent behavior is unproductive and detrimental to a skating program. Skaters, parents, and coaches all have a part in the skater's success and there will be times when the skater has setbacks. Setbacks are okay - they are life lessons and they help skaters to develop important life skills.

Other coaches have sided with this type of behavior in the past. They tell parents and skaters what they want to hear and act as though they have the power to fix all their problems in figure skating. I could write an entire book on the type of toxic atmosphere that this behavior causes in a rink. Coaches should be a team of professionals who support one another and teach parents that figure skating is a sport that requires hard work, discipline, and accountability. Coaches who search for disgruntled parents and offer to change their world with techniques but fail to teach the skaters responsibility and respect for coaches are like bottom feeders in a pond that thrive off mold.

When you love your work, it is hard to walk into a space where you know not everyone supports you and some people are waiting to see you fail. Perhaps you've experienced this in your career as a skater or coach. Unfortunately, there are more examples of this experience. My point is that coaching and directing is not always easy and there will be hurtful and discouraging encounters along the journey.

I wish someone had warned me more about this when I first became a coach. That way, I would have known to expect it but also feel prepared for the criticism. I've learned, when times are difficult, that the best thing to do is to remind myself why I love coaching. It also helps to have a strong support system that you can turn to in times of need, who can remind you that you love the sport and skaters you coach when you are about to hit send on that very detrimental email that can end it all. Also, it's a good idea to try to vow to make each decision with integrity so that, even when others are questioning your decisions, you know that you did the best you could.

Pleasing everyone is impossible but choosing to make the best decisions you can in each situation *is* possible. Your experience will differ from mine, but the takeaway is to build the educational and emotional tools to help persevere through those experiences and share those tools through your teachings with the skaters you work with.

# CHAPTER II

## BEFORE LESSONS BEGIN

*Choosing Skates*

"I found a pair of used skates online, so I ordered them." Cringe.

"I bought skates in my shoe size." Double cringe.

I hear these lines all the time. If I'm being completely honest, I did it myself a few years ago. I decided I was going to take on roller skating. A friend and I went to a sports store, and each bought a pair of skates for $25. The wheels were cheap, and the boots were flimsy, but I loved them. I can do a lot of the things that I do on the ice in them, but I know deep down that the figure skating coaches in roller skating would cringe at the sight of my skates showing up for a lesson.

Skating in supportive skates that fit correctly is *extremely* important for skaters. I am an advocate of new skaters wearing rentals until they decide if skating is a sport that they want to fully commit to, but I still prefer that they have a supportive pair of rentals that are not too big for them. This can be difficult since many new skaters expect skates to fit more like a pair of sneakers than a pair of heels. Skates should be tighter, fitted, and sometimes uncomfortable at first. Skates, like heels, have an adjustment period. Skates that are comfortable and not closely touching the skaters' feet are usually at least one size too big.

Choosing the skates to recommend to your skaters is largely based on preference, the logistics, and availability of brands in your area. Riedell is the most accessible brand in my area - unless you want a three-hour drive. I try to stay familiar with Riedell boot models to recommend to skaters based on skill level, age, and amount of time spent on the ice. However, there are other brands of boots that I personally prefer because of the success I have seen for skaters wearing them. I recommend other boots as skaters progress in their commitment to the sport and are willing to travel for skates.

Although I grew up in leather skates, it isn't always my first recommendation. They rot and break down more quickly. However, for young skaters with growing feet and beginner skaters who progress into firmer boots quickly, a leather boot is fine. The two things I look for in skates are: 1. whether they have a high heel (this naturally helps with deeper knee bends) and 2. whether they have a supportive tongue that also allows for flexibility. I prefer the tongue to move slightly with the skater's ankle, rather than the skater to have to push through tight laces to be able to bend.

There are so many types of blades to choose from. A very simple, basic blade is perfectly fine for someone who is just starting skating. A beginning blade will work if the blade has a rocker and sharpened edges. When skaters enter the free skate levels, I usually recommend a blade with a larger toe pick and a more curved rocker. Those help skaters with higher jumps, staying off their toe picks while traveling backwards, and finding their spin spots more easily.

Different coaches prefer certain brands of blades and, unlike boots where skaters need to be fitted in person, it seems very easy to order blades online from anywhere. Many of the websites for blades will have comparisons between brands and recommendations for certain levels which makes choosing the right blade for skaters simpler and more straightforward.

On the topic of blades, beginner skaters don't necessarily need blades to be sharpened at 7/16. Sharpenings at ½ inch are fine to begin with. Skaters transitioning into freestyle can start to look at deeper edges in their sharpenings over time.

*Lacing Skates*

The way in which a skater laces their skates can really help or hinder their abilities. Obviously, when skates are too loose, they can cause the ankles to wobble and balance to suffer. But skates that are too tight are bad for skaters as well. When skates are too tight, they constrict the skater's movement and they also can cause shin splints, lace bite, and other physical challenges.

Skaters should tie their own skates. (Read that sentence again. Then, please inform your skate families as quickly as you can). Skaters have an opportunity to learn independence in this sport and it's important for coaches to encourage this independence and recognize where certain behaviors can hinder children for many reasons. Skaters of all ages can take ownership of getting on the ice prepared and on time. I have spent many lessons next to the ice, teaching skaters how to lace their own skates and then giving them "homework" to practice the skill at home. It's so important that they know this and can get themselves ready for practice and lessons.

I usually give skaters and their families pointers on how to lace skates early on. Lacing skates properly is an important skill for them to have so that they can benefit from their skates rather than struggle because of them. One of the most important things I like skaters to know is that they should be able to fit two fingers inside the top of their laced boot. The laces around the foot should be snug and should not move when a finger runs over the top of them. The ankle should be the tightest part because it secures everything and holds the skate in place, with the skater's heel resting against the back of the boot.

The tongue of a skater's boots should allow room for the ankles to bend. When skaters tie the tongue of boots too snugly against their ankles, it constricts the joints from getting the proper bend and can cause the joints to work too hard against the laces to achieve the right amount of bend. As I mentioned, they should be able to fit 2-3 fingers between the top of the tongue of boot and their shin. The actual ankle joint, further down in their boot, should be tightly laced to provide support and help their heel to remain still in the boot.

There are many interesting things we see new skaters do when tying their skates. Sometimes laces drag along the ice, sometimes the top of the boot isn't tied at all, but the worst thing I see is when a skate's excess laces are wrapped around the top of the boot a few times. Those laces always travel over the boot and onto the leg of the skater and it is constricting but also dangerous. I recommend tucking in long laces instead.

*Parent Education*

I'm just going to leave a few words right here: chasse, compulsory, freestyle, USFS, swing roll, MK, test session, salchow, Riedell, scratch spin, PSA, back inside edge, snowplow stop, pre-preliminary, IJS, Edea, and 6.0. Those words probably made sense to you. But imagine reading those as a parent or a new skater; they would have absolutely no meaning.

Figure skating is a foreign language. Parents often look at me with a blank stare when I talk about some of these terms. I would expect them to at first. The good news is that parents don't have to know *every* detail about figure skating because they have the coaches to guide them about decisions and information regarding the sport. However, it is helpful for them to have a general understanding of what skaters are working toward and the way in which they can achieve those goals.

15

It is also important for a parent to understand what they *don't* know. Well-intentioned parents sometimes overstep their boundaries, either through various means of living or a belief that knowledge of another sport makes them an expert in figure skating. Sometimes, this comes up at the beginning of the coaching relationship (purchasing skating boots based on basketball shoe fit) and sometimes this issue comes up when parents don't hear what they want to hear.

One of the most difficult concepts to convey to parents is just how difficult figure skating is and that progress is based on time spent working on the ice rather than the passage of time itself. That is a very difficult concept for some parents (and skaters) to grasp. Parents will sometimes send a skater to practice once a week and then have unrealistic expectations of where their child should be after a year in skating. A year in skating can look very different for a skater who is at the rink everyday vs. one who is there once a week. Often, that needs to be explained to them.

I have had parents demand that it is time for a skater to test because months or a year has passed but the skater has not put in enough *quality* practice on the ice to be prepared for the test. It saves a lot of stress to let parents know upfront that there must be a consistent effort in order to see progress in a skaters' skills.

My years as an elementary school teacher taught me to be proactive about informing and educating parents. The worst experience is when you have bad news to report to a parent (e.g., their skater isn't ready for the upcoming test) and parents wonder why they are just now hearing the news. It's best to keep them informed along the way so that they don't receive sudden and surprising information and get upset.

In addition to understanding the goals for skaters and the amount of work that should go into achieving those goals, there are also some common areas of skating that parents generally have questions about, such as clean ice, freestyle sessions, and the role of the parent in the skaters' progress.

*Clean vs. Dirty Ice*

As skating director, I once had this conversation:

"I want a refund on Learn-to-Skate because the ice isn't clean. My daughter is very advanced in Basic 3 and she needs clean ice."

Pause, to process the advanced Basic 3 statement.

"She gets her skates sharpened in *Kansas City*. That dirty ice will ruin her blades."

Moment to cough and hide my laugh before responding as respectfully as possible. Unfortunately, this parent didn't know enough about skating to understand that her daughter's skates would survive dirty ice. I simply explained to her that dirty ice will *not* ruin blades and a skilled skater can skate on any type of ice and be fine.

Obviously, clean ice is preferred for most people but it's important for parents to understand that sometimes things go wrong: the zam stops working, the manager on duty has an emergency and can't get there to clean the ice, there was a special event, and more skaters were there than usual. And believe it or not, life goes on. As coaches, we can be a part of the problem or a part of the solution. Some coaches join in with parents and rile them up, but others choose to keep parents informed and help them to understand that their skater's blades will, in fact, survive ice that hasn't been cut.

In general, coaches sometimes must explain to skaters and parents that there will be "days like that" and they will make it. The life lessons in skating are never ending and learning to cope when conditions aren't perfect is a great life lesson for skaters. Skaters can still work on everything on dirty ice (or crowded ice) and it is good for them to experience it because there will be a day when they have to perform in a show or compete when the ice isn't clean.

*Public vs. Freestyle*

Parents and skaters don't always understand the difference between public and freestyle ice when they first start skating. It will be important for them to learn the rules of the ice for public and freestyle. They should also be instructed on whether they should practice on public or freestyle ice. Personally, I encourage skaters to practice on both sessions until they enter the free skate levels. When a skater reaches free skate, I expect them to practice on freestyle sessions to safely work on moves, edges, spins, and jumps.

Whether a coach decides to coach lessons on public or freestyle sessions is up to the coach and the rink policies. I used to coach on public ice, but I found that it is too dangerous and distracting for most skaters to have a lesson during public sessions. Freestyle ice gives skaters an opportunity to meet the other skaters at the rink, observe higher level skaters, and the opportunity to learn from role models about skills such as bringing water to the rink, warming up before skating, practicing independently, etc. Freestyles have overall been more effective for me; but the beauty of coaching and running your own business is that you get to make those decisions and policies independently based on what works best for you.

*Skater – Coach - Parent Triangle*

What I am about to say is the most important information in this book. If you decide you hate this book and want to throw it out, please just read this section first. Contrary to popular belief, the success of a skater is not dependent on how knowledgeable, strict, capable, talented, conceited, smart, etc. the coach is. I'm going to be honest; when I first started coaching, I sometimes made the mistake of thinking that. I blamed myself when skaters didn't progress or got injured and I praised myself when skaters soared through the levels and placed well in competitions. But it had very little to do with me: I was just along for the ride. I wish I had learned that sooner because it would have taken a lot of stress and pressure off me.

There are three parties involved in the success of a skater: the coach, the parent, and the skater. All three parties have roles to fulfill for positive progress to occur. It is not up to any of the three parts alone to create the progress. *The coach alone does not create progress.*

There will be skaters who put very little effort into practice but expect to progress and put all the pressure onto the coach for their progress to be made. Some skaters and parents believe coaches are magic genies who can wave their hands and skaters will land an axel. Likewise, there are coaches who advertise themselves as "the answer to figure skating" and they enable the lack of practice by telling parents what they want to hear. There is no quick and easy route in figure skating: there is hard work and effort from the parent, skater, and coach, equally.

The skater won't progress if the parent doesn't bring them to the lessons, to practice or support the coach and the skating process (adult skaters fill this parent role for themselves, so they have more responsibility for their own progress). Likewise, the skater won't progress if the coach doesn't believe in them or show up prepared for lessons. And, finally, the skater must be fully present during lessons and needs to mindfully practice with lots of effort both on and off the ice. If any part of the triangle is broken, the positive progress isn't there. The lessons become stagnant and eventually the skater burns out.

As shown in the figure above, the center of the triangle contains three key core values that all parties must encompass: commitment, accountability, and discipline. All three parties must be present and committed consistently. All three parties must be accountable for their actions, admit mistakes, and take ownership of their part in the progress. All three must be disciplined because progress emerges from discipline and the ability to step out of your comfort zone to improve.

No progress is made if the skater has a lazy day standing by the boards.

No progress is made if a coach stands with the skater chatting about summer vacation through the whole lesson.

No progress is made if the parent doesn't bring the skater to the rink for significant practice.

The three parts must work as a team and support one another while working toward common goals.

20

Okay, you can throw the book away now, if you really want. But please keep the skater, coach, parent triangle in mind especially because many of us will fill different roles of the triangle during different seasons in our lives and it's so imperative that we understand how it works, why it works, and that breaking it does not work, nor does it improve skater's abilities or accomplishments.

Parent Education Recap:

- There are a lot of terms parents won't understand: they don't need to know all of them, but they will need guidance from coaches, particularly about practice
- Be proactive about educating, especially when it comes to hard work and practice
- Remember that it takes equal effort from parent, skater, and coach for positive progress to occur

*Know your Worth*

When I first started coaching, my rate was $30/hour. Did your jaw just drop? Depending on where you live in the world, that probably sounds absurd. It *is* absurd. My current rate would probably sound equally laughable even though it has increased significantly. Unfortunately, in the area I coach, there is an atmosphere of "service" at the rink rather than "business." Many parents have come to expect coaches to be the answer to their needs and to give discounts and operate as cheaply as possible. Most of the coaches maintain that atmosphere by offering discounted competition and test sessions. As could be expected, this has created an environment where many skaters and parents do not have respect for coaches, and it is problematic.

This sport is expensive. Not only for skaters but for coaches as well. We have to pay for the skates, the coats, the hats, the never-ending hot hands, etc. A lot of rinks, including mine, charge a percentage for coaches to coach on their ice. Continuing education, insurance, and memberships are expensive to keep up with each

21

year, and, after all those expenses, a portion of the income is taken out for taxes. Not to mention that time is valuable and a significant amount of time for coaches is spent doing work outside of lessons (communicating with families, scheduling, planning programs and music, etc.).

People respect your time based on your rate. If your services are free or very cheap, people will often see you as unsuccessful or not worth hiring. I have witnessed parents at our rink expecting favors, discounts, and everything to be handed to them because they begin to see the coaching staff as there to personally serve them rather than as a group of professionals.

Know your worth. Remember that your time, skills, and experience are worthwhile, and you are within your rights to charge if you have to give up your weekend for a test session, show, or competition. You do not need to volunteer at your job, and you are not being selfish or acting as though you don't love the sport because you expect to be compensated for your time. Therefore, based on where you live and what the cost of living is in your area, I highly recommend charging a rate that is realistic, competitive, and well respected for your coaching skills.

*Lesson Policy*

An important part of coach education is sharing a lesson policy. This is a great way to start out on the same page as a team of skater-coach-parent. Some things that I have included in my lesson policy are my rate, any additional fees that I include (such as competition, test session, and music cutting fees), and my cancellation policy.

A few additional things that I include with my lesson policy are an accident waiver and I outline my expectations for skaters and families (e.g., respect skating community, communicate any issues directly to me, etc.). Since I share my expectations of skating families, I also find it helpful to share with them that they can expect

22

from me by including my mission statement. See chapter 12 on Coaching Philosophy to read more about developing a coach mission statement.

The great thing about being a coach is that you run your own business so you can really create your lesson policy to meet your needs and the needs in your area. For example, if paying on time is an issue in your rink then that would be something to include in the lesson policy. Lesson policies can be edited and updated as often as you need because you will probably find new issues pop up that need to be addressed for your business to run smoothly.

*Choose your People*

Coaches have just as much say in who they will work with on the ice as the skaters have in choosing their coaches. This is important if you prefer to surround yourself with skaters and families who demonstrate respectful behavior and realistic goals (goals in which the effort and time spent practicing match the desired outcome).

I've learned the hard way over the years that I can say no to working with certain skaters and families if we are not a good fit for one another. Since you are reading this, you probably have experience in the skating world and can think of your own examples. There are always people at the rink who will make demands of others and expect the rink/club/skating program/coaches to cater to them. Those are the people I avoid because they look for coaches who will serve them and tell them what they want to hear. Things usually don't end well when I get the sense that I am working with a family that doesn't respect others or my time, so I remind myself that it's okay to say "no" at any time. Skaters choose their coaches and coaches also choose their skaters.

# CHAPTER III

## BASIC SKILLS

*Skater's Should* Not *Bend Their Knees*

I sincerely hope you didn't throw this book across the room when you read that subtitle - although I would understand why you would. I may as well have just told you that the Earth is flat, or the Sun is not a star. "Bend your knees" is probably the single most used phrase by every coach across the world. And yet, if we truly examine this concept, we are not actually talking about knees bending at all: we are referring to ankles.

Don't believe me? Wherever you are, stand up and bend your knees but do so *without* bending your ankles. You may notice a slight movement – probably an inch or less- but nothing significant. Now bend your ankles. Did you notice the difference? You now have that full knee bend we look for in skaters. Instructing skaters to bring their awareness to the bend in their ankles has proven to be more effective for me than telling skaters to bend their knees.

Skaters need to experience what it *feels* like to bend their ankles in skates. If they can't feel the bend, they will only *think* they are bending. This challenge is comparable to the challenge of getting skaters to lock their knees when the free leg is extended. Skaters will demonstrate a locked knee position for their coach *thinking* their legs are straight when they are *actually* bent. For more details about what it feels like to *actually* lock your knee, refer to the sections on spinning and stroking.

To help skaters, understand knee bend, I ask them to tell me what they feel against their skin when they bend their ankles. It's simple – they'll notice the pressure of the tongue of their boots against their shins. Then, I instruct them to do whatever it is they are working on – whether they are practicing swizzles, slaloms, stroking, jump take offs, etc., while feeling the boot pressing against their shin to be sure that they are bending properly. Developing awareness of an external stimulus - the feeling of the tongue of the boot against their ankles- changes the outcome.

When I ask skaters to bend their ankles instead of their knees and they compare the two bends, I notice drastic changes in their skating. It's amazing to see the difference. When we change the wording and tell skaters to bend their ankles we get a much better knee bend from them, and better skating technique, by extension.

*The Breaking at the Waist Struggle*

When skaters don't bend their ankles and knees, the resulting effect is a break at the waist. Not bending at the knees and ankles causes skaters to bend too much at the hips and stick their bottoms out behind them, and they become unbalanced and have poor posture. When skaters begin their first lesson, skaters should stand with feet hip width apart, and bend their knees before moving so that they can work on the proper skating stance and avoid duck bottom. I also have them stand still and deliberately try breaking at the waist as well. It's helpful when skaters can feel the *wrong* position so that they will develop a body awareness and correct that position if they begin to skate in it.

One way that can help skaters remain aware of whether they look like skaters or ducks in the water with their tails in the air as they march and swizzle across the ice, would be to use their arms and hands for awareness. If they skate with their hands on their hips, they will be able to feel whether their hips are bending too much as they focus on their knee and ankle bends instead. I also like to position because it helps align shoulders on top of hips when skaters are at an early stage and can't necessarily maintain that posture as well with their arms out to the side.

25

Skater Stance Recap:

- Stand with feet in skates, shoulder width apart
- Bend knees and ankles; don't break at the waist
- Try practicing the wrong position to see how different it feels

*Discovering Blades*

New skaters should be introduced to the details going on beneath their feet so that they can have some awareness and control of the blade from the beginning. I start every beginner class by having skaters get familiar with their blades. It's important for them to understand that blades are not flat and that we have two edges and a toe pick on blades. It's also fun to ask new skaters what they think we use toe picks for on the ice. A *surprising* number of people think they are for stopping or spinning.

Beginner skaters discover how their blades rock by putting their weight on one foot and moving their other blade slowly forward and backward. This will help a new skater notice that not all parts of the blade are on the ice at once, but rather, it operates more like a rocking chair, depending on where they are placing pressure on their foot and where the skate is in relation to their hips. After they are comfortable with that motion, they can try standing with weight evenly distributed between both hips and slowly rock their hips forward and backward, feeling both blades rock together.

Skaters may notice they stand with more weight rocked towards the front of their blades as they gently glide backward on the ice, and they will have more weight towards the heel of their blades as they gently glide forward. I tell skaters that the front of their blade is their "reverse button" on the ice. (If you've ever seen a young skater march in place and go nowhere but look like they are trying to climb up an icy hill, it is because of this concept – skaters press toward the front of the blade while moving backward and the back of the blade while moving forward).

Next, I have skaters hold the wall, put their weight on one foot, and lean the other foot (without weight on it to protect their ankles) slowly towards the outside and move it backward and forwards to feel the grip of the outside edge. Then they can do the same thing with the inside edge by tilting their foot slightly inwards. I explain to them that we have two edges on each blade, and we skate on one or the other much of the time. Some of these concepts may sound simple to those of us who have been on the ice for a long time but it's something that can be overlooked and needs to be explained to new skaters.

Finally, I have skaters stand and place their weight on one foot again and lift and bend the other knee, bringing the toe pick under their hip so that they can feel it. If they are comfortable with this and with balancing on the ice, some skaters can even walk on their toe picks early on in skating. Skaters who do this successfully notice how they must point their toes, press their hips forward, and straighten their knees to maintain the correct position.

It's also fun for skaters to walk sideways on toes by taking small steps and shifting their weight while side-stepping. They can also walk backwards on their toes. Skaters can perform half turns on their toes by lifting one foot and pivoting the standing leg until they have turned 180 degrees and then set their other foot beneath them and continue turning in the same direction. The key is keeping their feet under their hips, so they are always balanced on top of their toe picks.

Developing an understanding of the mechanics of blades helps skaters to remain aware of the connection between their feet and the ice and have better control in their skating overall.

Discovering Blades Recap:

- Discover that blades can rock by rocking forward and backward
- Set toe picks until hips - walk on them if comfortable
- Hold the wall and lean foot (without weight) onto edges

*Marching*

Skaters who are afraid of the ice may struggle with marching across the ice because they are fearful of standing on one foot. Before they march across the ice, skaters should be able to stand with feet hip-width apart and practice shifting their weight from one hip to the other without lifting their feet. This can be done by bending into one knee and shifting hips over that knee and then switching to the other. Skaters can imagine they are putting their belly button and nose (since those help them visualize their center) over one hip and then the other.

Once skaters are comfortable with this, they can try to march in place. It's important to notice *how* they should bend and *how* they must transfer their weight from one hip to the other to lift one foot. We do this naturally off the ice while walking, but new skaters must think about it more on the ice, particularly if they are afraid (the fear barrier is a difficult one to break down but breaking down the mechanics of things into simple parts assists the process for skaters).

New skaters have spent their entire lives walking and will often skate as though they are walking in shoes (they set one foot in front of the other and that foot reaches out in front of their hips instead of keeping boots beneath hips).

While marching forward, skaters continue to practice proper blade awareness by pressing down into their feet to maintain power and, more specifically, by pressing into the center/back of their

28

blade. This is the spot that we often naturally press when stomping down with our feet and skaters will press the center back of the foot anytime they are skating forward.

There are several other skills that skaters can practice while marching forward across the ice. One skill is to train their eyes to look forward and, by extension, skating with their heads up. Skaters can find a spot on the wall across the ice to focus their eyes on as they skate. When they focus on what their feet are doing, skaters tend to look down at the ice, but skating is a feeling sport, and it is never too early to train skaters to feel their feet and keep their eyes up.

Another skill skaters can work on during marching is posture. If skaters keep their core engaged while skating forward, it will help them with their balance and posture. It's important to note that it isn't just a skater's abs that maintain balance while skating, but their backs as well. Keeping their backs straight (not arched) and shoulder blades pinched together can help with balance.

Marching Recap:

- Begin by marching in place and shifting weight from one hip to the other
- Weight should be toward the center-back of the blade
- Have skaters practice keeping their eyes up and focused on something
- Skaters should keep their backs straight and core engaged for balance

*Falling is Good - Falling Poorly is Not*

Falls can be rough. But I still love them, and I am encouraged by my falls (although I don't always enjoy them) and I love it when the skaters I coach fall. It's a good thing when skaters start tripping more often on an element they are working on because

29

falls mean progress: a skater falls when they step out of their comfort zone.

Ice falls are often represented in pop culture [think Ice Princess, The Cutting Edge, etc..] as a bad thing but I see them as a positive. However, I do think that safe falling should be taught. There is more benefit in relaxing during a fall and falling to the side than panicking and tensing muscles or falling backwards with their hands behind them (broken arms are a frequent injury of beginner skaters trying to protect their backsides on the way down).

I broke my ankle when I panicked during a fall. To be fair, I was on a busy freestyle, in the ice rink that I like to refer to as a fishbowl, with parents and skaters watching from all around. The pressure of being a coach and falling on a three-turn caused me to tense up during the fall and I ended up injured. I'll never be positive about whether being tense caused me to break my ankle, but I do know it was something that happened during the fall and that could have been a factor. Due to that, I am a fan of teaching skaters to relax and accept a fall whenever one comes knocking.

It's also important for skaters to rehearse certain steps to take after they fall. Not sitting on the ice is a big thing. It may sound obvious, but I see it all the time and it scares me to think of how easily a skater could be tripped over while sitting on the ice. Allowing their skates to go to one side, away from their body is another good thing to consider. Not a fan of falling with two giant knives close to me, so the further away they go, the better. Skaters should be aware of protecting their fingers by pulling their arms in close to their bodies immediately after falling - for obvious reasons. And, finally, I like to remind skaters to tuck their chins when they fall, to protect their heads from hitting the ice.

Falling Recap:

- Safe falling is encouraged
- Skaters should relax and tuck their chins while falling

- Skaters should get up quickly after falling

*Arms up - but not all the way*

Skaters at the beginner levels learn all the different pieces that go into balancing on the ice. Requiring skaters to hold their arms at shoulder height does not necessarily need to be one of them (unpopular opinion, I know, but hear me out on this one). Skaters over time use their backs to hold their arms up by pinching their shoulder blades together to maintain their posture. I do think it's important for skaters to practice this as they learn to march across the ice and do swizzles, etc., but new and untrained skaters will tend to lift their arms with the top of their arm muscles. This will cause the muscles to become sore and tired, and it takes away from the focus on their ankles, backs, knees, blade pressure, etc.

If you ever had an off-ice class where you hold your arms up for a minute or more and feel the stinging pain (very effective workout) you can relate to what the poor basic 1 skaters feel as they march back and forth across the ice, trying to balance but also being told to put their arms up every few minutes. It seems like an exhausting distraction from what really matters and a quick way to stomp out the love for skating very early on. Instead, beginner skaters can try to hold their arms *out*. That means they can be reaching for balance, but they can be low, more like table height, if needed.

Additionally, skaters can practice swizzles with their hands on their hips. It is a more comfortable position for them, and it brings awareness to their hips so that they can feel whether they are bending their knees or bending their hips and preventing breaking at the waist.

*Swizzles and Slaloms*

Swizzles and slaloms are everything on the ice. And I mean *everything*. Swizzles and slaloms are two of the most important

31

things taught in figure skating because they connect to everything; leaning, bending, pressure into ice, posture, and proper ankle rhythm, to name a few. Skaters begin to learn the correct technique for these from day one and should work on them throughout all their years in figure skating.

*Sloppy Swizzles*

Even long-time freestyle skaters often become sloppy with swizzles and should review the technique and practice them regularly/use them for warm-ups. Nothing is ever too simple to relearn, because, as their skills progress, they will be able to add more mastery to each skill, no matter how basic the skill. Often when skaters are struggling with a jump, spin, or difficult step or turn, it can be traced to a very simple issue that comes from the basics. The basic levels contain the most critical elements and should continue to be a part of every skater's practice throughout their development.

*Swizzles and Hip Rotation*

Swizzles help skaters learn internal and external hip rotation which they will use for just about everything, whether it is their free leg or skating leg being rotated on the ice. For example, they will rotate externally on their stroking pushes, rotate internally on their salchow take-offs, and rotate externally when going into a sit or camel spin. If a skater holds an internally rotated swizzle position on the ice and lifts one leg, keeping it rotated inward, they will find themselves in their h-position for jumps. Therefore, this skill is crucial to their skating skills, and it usually begins to form on their first day of skating.

The first thing I like to show skaters, when learning swizzles in Basic 1, is how to stand still and simply rotate their hips open and closed. Many skaters will struggle with keeping their feet under their hips and getting their heels and toes to touch, but it is important they are able to achieve this before moving across the ice doing swizzles.

The external rotation is very connected to "First Position" in ballet. However, we don't spend a lot of time off the ice simply rotating our hips open and closed in everyday life, so this is a technique skaters need to feel and to practice. Often, one direction is more difficult for skaters, and it is dependent on each person and body type whether their hips rotate externally or internally more naturally. Off-ice stretching, and exercises help skaters with this and it's never too early to begin working on these skills off the ice.

In addition to learning hip rotation, swizzles also challenge skaters to press into the ice to generate power and teach them how to bend properly and stand with correct skating posture. Knees and ankles don't remain bent during swizzles; there is an ankle bend *and* rise rhythm that takes place during swizzles that skaters will use in all areas of skating. Skaters should enter each swizzle with a bend to load the muscles, then they should rise (by pushing down) in order to create power during the second half of the swizzle (the part when their hips are closing, and toes move together). The second half of the swizzle is the part that generates the most power.

*Pushing down* is crucial. Pushing up creates less power. Skaters should try standing still and bending and rising simply by lifting their heads up as if someone is pulling them upward. This type of pushing up does not generate as much power on the ice. Next, they should rise in their knees the correct way, in which they rise by pressing down into their feet. The pressure into the ice causes a skater's knees and ankles to straighten. This feels very different from the first time they stood up by simply lifting. This comparison exercise is useful in future turns, jump take offs, and pressing onto the ball of the foot in spins.

Many skaters swizzle across the ice without the proper technique while keeping their legs very straight. Sometimes, skaters feel frustrated by taking the time to learn the bend and pressing into the ice method, but it is crucial that they develop the skill early since it will affect the rest of their skating skills. Skaters can try the straight-legged swizzle on purpose, to see how little power they gain and then try one from a standstill where they begin by bending into their ankles. The second way should feel much more powerful, although more difficult at first. Skaters bend and feel the tongue of the boot against their skates. While standing still, just bending causes them to glide forward on the ice. As their hips internally rotate, they should rise in their knees by pressing down into the ice, feeling their speed increase as they press.

*Slaloms - an Introduction to Leaning*

Slaloms are introduced in later introductory classes (Basic 3) but skaters can start practicing curving from side to side before they are officially introduced. Curves teach skaters how to lean, how to feel their edges, and how to create pressure into the ice. Let's begin with lean. Almost everything we do on the ice requires us to lean. Leans feel very natural to those of us who have been skating for years, but, to anyone new to skating, their brain is registering that they are standing sideways, and gravity can pull them down. People often resist the lean automatically. This resistance is purely out of instinct.

New adult skaters tend to do this the most because they have spent more time in life fighting the effects of gravity. They have had courses in physics, witnessed (and probably experienced) injuries to varying degrees, and they recognize what could go wrong. The fear is valid but recognizing it and working through the fear is necessary for progress.

A lot of time and practice should go into teaching skaters how it feels to lean on the ice and that we gain power on the ice by achieving this "almost falling" posture. Skaters can practice leaning by placing both hands on the wall, then rotating their hips under them 90-degrees so that their feet are parallel to the wall. They can then lean their ankle, knee, and hips, focusing on total alignment of the legs (rather than isolating the hip or ankle) and feel how they stand only on one side of their blade while moving one blade forward and backward slowly.

During forward slaloms, skaters change edges each time they enter a new lobe, while making an "s" pattern down the ice. The blades are both on opposite edges the whole time: during a lobe, the inside foot leans on an outside edge and the outside foot leans on an inside edge, then they switch edges for the new lobe. The knee rhythm during slaloms is a constant down, up motion, in which the skater bends the most at the first half of the lobe and then rises and speeds up with increased blade pressure for the second half of the lobe.

Skaters keep their feet directly beneath hips and maintain a strong upper body position in slaloms. It's easy for skaters to get sloppy and break at the waist, so they must focus on keeping their backs straight and eyes looking forward. Another important aspect to slaloms is the opposite shoulder to hips motion. Skaters' shoulders face the direction of travel the entire time a skater does slaloms, even though skaters' hips rotate from one direction to the other. This is because skaters rotate their shoulders opposite their hips so that their hips face one direction, but their shoulders continue to face in the direction they are skating. This shoulder against hip motion can also contribute to having powerful and controlled slaloms.

*What is "Checking?"*

I ask skaters all the time whether they know what it means "to check" and not just in chess (which, by the way, I have *no idea* what it means "to check" in chess). I *check in* with skaters about this concept often because, when I was young, my coach used to constantly yell at me *to check my shoulders* and I had no clue what she meant so I just flailed around doing things until she said, "That's it!" It can be a bit surprising how many skaters (and coaches) do not truly understand the concept of checking. Some people think

35

checking means rotating arms from one side to the other, but that alone does nothing to help control edges. If we help skaters to understand the concept of what checking truly is, then they will be better at applying the position to their turns, jumps, crossover patterns, etc. and checking will have a huge impact on their quality of skating.

"To check" simply means this: rotating shoulders against hips to control rotation. Skaters need to turn their torso 45 degrees in order to achieve a proper checked position. One way I have them try this is by resting their arms by their sides (so that they can't just turn their arms and think they are checked) and then have them rotate their upper body one direction until their chest is directly over their right hip or over their left hip. Once they achieve this rotation, they can lift their arms to shoulder height, stretch them out in a straight line, and notice where their arms are, following the line of their shoulders.

*"Checking" Exercises*

Another way for skaters to experience this checked upper body rotation is to stand still and rotate their shoulders and lay both hands on one hip, with their chest turned enough so that it is directly above their hip. They can then open their arms and see how they create a straight line, where one arm reaches directly out from the front shoulder and one reaches directly out from the back shoulder, because the torso is twisted. Holding a hockey stick and rotating their torso so that the hockey stick rotates over one hip then the other is also effective.

This exercise is useful during 3-turns as well: skaters perform a 3-turn, beginning with their hands stacked (elbows apart) on the inside hip, rotated into the turn, and then, as they turn their hips under them during the turn, they rotate shoulders the other direction so that their hands rest on the other hip; the hip that is now inside the lobe. For example, for a right forward outside three-turn, skaters will begin with their hands on their right hip and then turn at the top of the lobe and switch hips so that their shoulders are over their left hip and their hands rest on their left hip.

Skaters also benefit from experiencing the opposite of checking and the lack of control that goes with it. If they struggle to understand why checking is important, I instruct them to try a turn in which their shoulders just simply move with their body, wherever it feels natural during the turn. Usually, the resulting turn feels out of control for skaters, and they realize that they need to be checking their shoulders for control.

Checking Recap:

- Skaters often think checking means rotating their arms
- Checking is turning shoulders against hips to control rotation
- Skaters can practice this position at a standstill to understand that their torso needs to be rotated 45 degrees (chest over hip)
- Have skaters try *not checking* their shoulders in turns to experience the difference and understand the importance of checking

## Two-Foot Turns

Two-foot turns introduce skaters to several skating concepts, one of which is checking, or moving hips and shoulders in opposite directions during a turn to control the rotation. I like to use the line when first teaching two-foot turns to provide skaters a visual of how far a 180-degree turn rotates. (The 180-degree turn is a great example of how educational skating can be in teaching math, geometry, and physics). When skaters turn a full 180 degrees, they will notice that their feet line up on the line facing the opposite direction that they started. Often, skaters will struggle with making a full 180 degree turn at first, but I will include some tips to help with that.

Skaters begin with both feet on the line, hip-width apart, with hips, knees, and toes facing one wall of the rink. They rotate their arms and shoulders so that they are not square to their hips but are rotated to the side (checked). I have skaters practice the *bend, rise, bend* motion in their ankles and try to turn their hips so that their feet rotate to face the opposite side of the rink. Usually, at this point, skaters have discovered the rock on their blade and can practice bending and then straightening their knees and rocking slightly forward toward the front of the blade. They will probably do this in a few short, jagged motions at first, as they turn in the middle of their blade, and it scrapes. Eventually, skaters figure out that they will rock to the ball of their foot during the turn when their legs are locked and hips rock forward.

One helpful tool is to practice these turns on an area of clean ice so skaters can look at the ice after they turn to see if they created snow or not. If they created snow, then they are not rocking forward enough and putting weight on the front of the blade properly.

Next, skaters need to be sure that they turn their upper bodies the opposite direction as their hips rotate. This ensures a full 180-degree turn. They should practice rotating fully from one direction to the next until they are able to do so quietly on the blade, in one swift motion, and with a proper checked position. Often, skaters will move one foot and have the other foot follow, so it's important they can practice having both feet move as one during a two-foot turn. Sometimes, imagining that both feet are tied together and squeezing toward one another can help skaters who struggle with keeping their feet together.

*The Dance*

As skaters get more comfortable with two-foot turns, I like to introduce what I call "The Dance" across the line. To give a visual of this, it looks something like the old Intermediate bracket pattern (yes, I skated in the days of that pattern). If you aren't familiar with it, skaters turn their skating foot quickly forward and backward while moving across the ice, performing brackets. However, the dance drill is simplified and done on two feet, without using edges. This drill allows skaters to practice rocking for two-foot turns in both directions.

Here's how the dance goes: skaters begin at a standstill and perform a two-foot turn. Then, instead of rotating the other direction and staying in one place turning back and forth, they keep their shoulders in the same place and turn from backward to forward. Continuing down the line, skaters will turn from backward to forward then forward to backward. The turn from backward to forward is initiated by rising in the knees and pressing on the heel of the blade, instead of the ball of the foot.

As skaters perform this drill, their upper bodies face the same direction the entire time as they move down the line. For example, a skater can begin with a counter-clockwise forward two-foot turn and continue with a clockwise backward two-foot turn, then repeat the first turn again, and so forth, across the ice. When this drill is done properly with enough pressure applied to the blade, skaters move continuously down the line because they glide backward and forward in between each turn as they rock to the ball of their feet and then rock to the heel of their feet. There is a constant bend, rise, bend pattern in the ankles, in which skaters bend before and after the turn but rise during each turn. Skaters end up looking as though they are performing a dance move across the ice. This can be used in choreography as well.

*Two-Foot Turns on the Circle*

Two-foot turns on the circle are performed the same as standstill turns but they incorporate edges and leaning into the turn, which better prepares skaters for three-turns. Skaters begin by performing counterclockwise pumps on the circle and gliding on two edges while leaning into the circle, noticing that their left foot is leaning on an outside edge while their right foot is leaning on an inside edge. Ankles bend during the edge and skaters keep weight in the middle back of their blades.

Once skaters can hold this position and keep their shoulders rotated into the circle, they can try the moving turn. Skaters begin the turn with a knee bend and by rotating shoulders more strongly into the circle. Skaters' shoulders rotate as their hips rotate, and they should immediately bend after turning and keep leaning into their circle. Holding the edge after the turn is sometimes difficult, so they need to remember to keep their head looking in the direction of travel for control. Skaters can repeat this turn in the opposite direction, keeping in mind that one direction will be more difficult than the other and will require extra practice.

*Two-Foot Turns Recap*

- Two-foot turns should be quiet and not scrape the ice or cause snow
- Skaters check shoulders during two-foot turns
- Forward to backward two-foot turns rock to the ball of the foot and backward to forward two-foot turns rock to the heel of the foot.
- Skaters should keep their heads still, looking in the direction of travel throughout the entire two-foot turn

*Three-Turns Matter A LOT*

Have you ever noticed that everything we do in skating is a three-turn? It is one of the most interesting parts of the sport for me. We enter all spins from three-turns. All jumps are simple three-turns in the air (and we begin many jumps with three-turns during take-offs). A lot of our other turns on the ice either enter or exit the turn in a three-turn position (rotated into the circle if traveling forward and rotated outside of the circle if traveling backward). Often, our free leg will perform a "three-turn in the air" so that a complicated step like any of the Mohawks, or Choctaws can be made possible. A "three turn in the air" refers to the hip, foot, and knee rotating inward when moving from forward to backward or rotating outward when moving from backward to forward.

Three-turns truly depict a skater's quality of skating. Through a three-turn, you can observe a skater's proper edge placement and weight distribution on the blade. A three-turn will also highlight the bend and rise in the ankle and knees that should be both soft and rhythmic, the ability to create power when exiting a turn, proper posture including shoulders back, head placement, and not breaking at the waist.

In skating, there are eight three-turns: the forward outside on each foot, forward inside on each foot, backward outside on each foot, and backward inside on each foot. Skaters tend to have better three-turns when turning the direction in which they spin and rotate jumps. For example, a skater who rotates counter-clockwise, will naturally be stronger at left forward outside three-turns, right forward inside three-turns, right backward outside three-turns, and left backward inside three-turns (if anyone is ever actually *naturally stronger* in back inside three-turns, I don't know. I haven't seen that yet. The challenges with weight placement on back inside three turns, makes them the most difficult three turns to master).

Skaters check shoulders during three-turns and must check strongly into their turn directly *before* turning to help set the turn and then check in the other direction *during* the turn to control the turn. The shoulder checked position that we use in three-turns has everything to do with proper crossover positions, spins, and, quite possibly most importantly, jumps. But we'll get to that later.

Skaters should keep heads still during a turn and constantly look in the direction of travel. Skaters tend to move their head with their hips while turning, and there is so much more control when their head never moves during a forward three-turn. During a backward three-turn, skaters can turn their heads to look behind them (outside of the circle) before the turn so that they do not have to turn their heads while their hips turn. We maintain a lot of our balance from our head remaining still so keeping it still during a turn has a strong impact on the edge being smooth. Try a turn in which you move your head and one in which your head doesn't move - the difference is amazing.

*Ankle Rhythm in Three-Turns*

It's important for skaters to review two-foot turns before learning three-turns to be sure they check properly, keep their head still during the turn, and use proper ankle rhythm to rock on the blade during the turn. Ankles bend the most just *before* and *after* a turn and skaters rise in their ankles and knees *during* the turn. This rise in the knees promotes a fluid, soft turn which also takes pressure off the blade as the skater gently rocks to the turning spot on the blade (front of the blade for forward turns and heel of the blade for backward turns).

Three-Turns Recap:

- Execute the bend-rise-bend motion (turn during the rise)
- Skaters should check shoulders during their turn (rotate shoulders one direction and hips the other)
- Skaters should keep head still during a turn and constantly look in the direction of travel
- When they rock properly on the blade, the turn will feel natural and light to skaters

*Forward Stroking*

There are many key skills involved in forward stroking. Most skaters are first introduced to the concept of forward stroking in Basic 2 with scooter pushes. Scooter pushes teach skaters to work on the ways to create power with a stroking push as well as the proper stance and posture necessary for stroking. Because skaters push continuously with the same foot (as

42

if they are riding a scooter), they can practice power and posture without the shift of weight between hips that you normally see in forward stroking. This provides an excellent opportunity to have skaters bend their ankles, keep their backs straight, and extend their free legs.

*Pointing Toes*

Forward stroking is usually one of the first times that we address toe points on the ice. I find it's important to not just tell skaters to point their toes but to discuss what it *feels like* to point their toes in skates. The feeling is very different in skates versus out of skates. Try pointing your toes when you're not wearing shoes or skates and notice how your ankle stretches into a long, straight position, but your foot also rounds, and your toes stretch farther from your ankle. We often think of pointing in terms of that long stretch through our foot and the curving in our arch, but it isn't possible to point in skates that way.

The motion of pointing our toes is much smaller in skates but it is still an important movement. Skaters move their ankle joint a few inches so that their toe stretches *away* from their ankle. The best way for skaters to find awareness in whether they are pointing their toes is by tuning in to the back of their boots in the place where the top of the boots rest against their calf muscles. Remember, when bending, or flexing, the ankle, skaters feel the tongue of their boots pushing against their shins. They should also *not* feel the back of their boot against their calf muscles at this point. But, when pointing toes, skaters should feel the back of the boot pressing against their calves. Skaters are not pointing their toes enough if they don't feel that pressure against the calf.

Skaters who struggle to point their toes on the ice often struggle because they don't know what the point should feel like. A helpful exercise for skaters is to hold the wall, extend their free leg, and practice pointing and flexing in each boot, to feel the difference. Awareness is everything.

43

Some skates, like dance boots, allow more space to point toes because of a lower cutout in the heel. Skaters in dance boots can stretch their ankle longer with the result of a more pointed toe. Regardless of how low the cutout in the back of the boot is, skaters should always feel it against their calves when pointing. (Please refer to more information about boots in chapter two).

## Blade Pressure and Positioning in Stroking

During stroking, skaters' blade pressure remains in the middle-back of the blades. That means they feel like they are balanced over their arches and heels. A skater struggles with staying back on the blades when the skater allows the upper body to lean forward.

The stroke is performed correctly when there is sufficient knee and ankle bend to keep a skater's weight on the back of the blade. A sure sign that a skater's weight is too far forward is the toe pick trip that sends a skater flying forward. One way that skaters can practice staying in the middle back of their blade is by stomping their feet (either in place or moving). The spot where skaters feel pressure in the boot when they stomp (arches and heels) is the spot they should push down on while stroking. Discovering this stomping spot can help skaters to become aware of where to stand and to keep pressure in that spot.

## Edges or Flats?

It seems like a lot of skaters perform forward strokes on flats instead of edges. Skating is all about edges and, stroking, as something skaters do frequently, should be done on edges. A few years ago, I coached a few adult skaters on stroking with edges instead of just on flats. They had skated for a couple of years. As they pushed onto edges when they stroked, they-were amazed at how much easier it was to grip the ice with their blades. The edges also help skaters to feel more balanced.

You're probably wondering if stroking should be done on outside or inside edges. The short answer is- both. Skaters can begin by pushing onto shallow outside edges. During the stroke, they can shift gradually to inside edges to take them back to the axis so they can continue down the ice in a relatively straight line. If this is new information, I strongly recommend trying stroking this way next time you're on the ice.

The position during forward stroking is uncomfortable. I tell skaters all the time that if they feel relaxed during stroking then they aren't doing it correctly. The free hip turns out and the glutes squeeze and extend so that the free leg is stretched at a 45-degree angle and lifted high. The toes are pointed, and knees are locked. Skaters should feel their shoulders squeeze together, pressing down as they lengthen through their spine and neck.

Forward Stroking Recap:

- Skaters bend their ankles when initiating a forward stroke to load the muscles and create pressure into the ice
- Skaters lock their knees and *point their toes* during the push for proper carriage and power
- Skaters balance their weight over the middle-back of their blades
- Stroking is performed on shallow edges instead of flats

*Edges: Lean like a Hockey Stick*

There have been so many instances where I have asked a skater to hold an edge and they have proceeded to go in a circle (while struggling) on a flat. Skaters often believe that they are on an edge simply because they are traveling in a circle. The challenge is to find ways to show them the actual feeling of an edge vs. a flat.

The first thing to understand is the blade will be at an angle (shallow or deep) when skaters are on a true edge. Either their big toe or little toe will be closest to the ice, depending on which edge they are holding. Edges begin with the foot: skaters feel as though they are standing on one edge of their foot with very little to no pressure on the opposite side of their foot. This weight placement is very slight; they should think about the center of their foot and just move their weight slightly toward the pinky toe or big toe side for outside or inside edges. They should be in tune with their skate enough that they become aware of this change in foot pressure as they skate.

It's important for skaters to understand that they should *not* achieve this lean in their foot by rolling their ankles and isolating the lean to just their foot. This is bad for alignment. Skaters also should avoid holding an edge by pressing their hip out, into the circle. Instead, skaters should have the boot and blade angled and the rest of their body should follow with good alignment. In other words, a skater's ankle, knee, and hip should all line up and lean as one. I often use a hockey stick as an example by holding it next to a skater and leaning it one direction. I tell skaters their hips, knees, and ankles should lean the same way the hockey stick leans all as one, without any part popping out and leaning on its own.

Skaters sometimes understand what *not* to do when they try something incorrectly (if safety isn't an issue). Skaters can experience an incorrect edge by staying centered on the flat of their blade while traveling in a circle. Often a skater's blade will skid when they do this, and the skater will feel out of control. Usually when a skater tries an incorrect edge purposefully, the skater can recognize that it feels wrong and will know what a true edge feels like instead.

That way, they can correct themselves during practice. And isn't teaching all about teaching independence, anyway?

# CHAPTER IV

## TRANSITIONING SKILLS TO MOVES IN THE FIELD

Moves in the field provide a strong structure for a skater's overall abilities and impact other areas of skating such as jumping, spinning, choreography, and dance. Moves depict skaters' true abilities on the ice and are created to challenge skaters so they can't hide their weaknesses but instead, must push through them in order for the test to be ready.

For example, skaters may have a spiral that is stronger on one foot than the other, but they have to skate both spirals correctly in order to pass the first test. A skater may also be able to do a quick three-turn in each direction, but, when asked to hold the edges and follow a pattern using the other three-turn, flaws like toe scraping, hips dropping, and lack of checking will become apparent. The challenges that skaters have to overcome on each test are amazing ways to push them past their previous limits and open up doors to new levels of skating.

Before moves in the field, skaters used to take figures tests. Figures pushed skaters' edge abilities to high standards. During the time of figures, skaters demonstrated excellent control and awareness of their blades. I have bittersweet memories of the early morning "patch" sessions when skaters would each work on their circles on their section of ice, going over edges for what felt like an eternity. Figures takes a lot of dedication, but the edge outcome is worthwhile. There are some figures patterns in the moves in the field tests, such as the forward and backward circle 8s. The figures patterns are often the ones I see skaters struggle with the most in each test.

Before diving into the details on moves in the field skills, I want to share some information about the test levels and timelines for testing. There are eight levels of moves in the field standard tests, each with at least four patterns in the test. There are four levels of adult tests. The amount of time it takes to prepare for a test varies, depending on several factors.

The first factor is the skater's work ethic. As discussed in chapter one, skaters will progress based on the amount of quality practice time spent on the ice, not the amount of time that passes. It's difficult for me to tell skaters that they can be ready to pass a test in a number of months or years because the progress is measured in the effort they put forth. I estimate that it takes about a year to prepare for a test, for a skater who is consistently practicing. It will also vary depending on the test. The tests become more difficult as skaters move up and they can take longer to master.

A second factor as to the timeline for testing is the coach's preference. As a coach, I personally prefer skaters not to rush tests because skating isn't an instantaneous sport: it takes hard work and dedication to improve. When skaters rush through the first few tests, they often have weak tests in the higher levels because the skill mastery just isn't there. The greatest things in life take time and effort and moves in the field tests teach skaters great lessons in dedication, patience, and hard work.

To pass a moves test is a great accomplishment since the work leading up to the test is rigorous. Additionally, to pass *all* of the tests and become a gold medalist is an accomplishment that deserves the utmost respect. Many skaters set out to achieve that goal and few actually make it. The tests require patience in the process as well as intense practice.

48

*Alternating Edges on the Line*

Let's begin with edges since they are the foundation of all things in skating. If a skater can't hold a controlled edge, they will struggle with most things on the ice. It is important for new skaters (and families) who think they've "already learned edges" to understand why continued work on fundamentals is an important practice of figure skating.

There is so much to say about the alternating edge pattern in Pre-Preliminary. Skaters are introduced to these patterns at a very minimal level in Learn-to-Skate, but the standards for testing and working through these patterns for testing moves are different. The push for all four edges (forward outside, forward inside, backward outside, and backward inside) will be used in every single moves test in the future.

I frequently have skaters working on higher level tests return to the alternating edges on the line pattern to strengthen their pushes, because it's amazing how quickly skaters like to return to toe-pushing.

*Keep the Train Going*

Skaters pass their arms very closely by their sides when they switch their arms so that everything remains still and centered over the edge. This may seem like an easy concept, but skaters need to practice standing still to really feel their fingertips brush by their hips as they switch arms. Skaters can also practice the edges on two feet and just focus on their posture and arms passing close by their sides either at the top of the lobe or ⅔ of the lobe.

The back arm can even press down behind the skater so that it feels as though the palm is resting on something behind the skater. I often follow skaters and have them press their back palms into mine as they skate so that they feel themselves pushing down against something. When they switch arms, they should feel the new back arm pushing down just the same as the original one was pushing.

Skaters should keep their free leg close to their skating leg while holding these edges. When skating forward, a skater usually tucks the free foot behind the skating foot then moves it carefully in front of their foot during the lobe. While skating backward, a skater usually begins with the free foot extended in front and then slides it behind the skating foot at the top of the lobe. When a skater passes the free foot, it should rub so closely against the skating foot that it begins to scuff up the boots. This skill is hard for skaters to recognize so I like to have them practice it while holding the wall first.

I sometimes refer to a skater's two feet as two different cars on a train. They have to line the train cars up correctly on the track in order to hold the edge properly (this is a figures skill that I picked up). This means the free leg is locked and extended forward and the free foot is pointed and traveling slightly above but in line with the skating foot.

*Hips Don't Lie*

Holding an edge on a tiny blade while balancing on ice is not easy, despite how easy skaters can make it look. There are several small things that skaters can do that make their edges easier to hold, and overall cleaner.

The placement of a skater's hips is crucial to edges. The skating hip should be tucked under their torso, lined up with their knee and ankle. A common misconception for skaters is that they should pop their hip out, leaning it into the circle to maintain a true edge. While it's true the skating hip should lean into the circle, it should be lined up on top of the knee and ankle and they should all lean as one.

In any outside edge (forward or backward), a skater's free hip should be lifted higher than the skating hip and stacked so that the weight of the free hip is over the skating side. In any inside edge (forward or backward), a skater's free hip should be held level with the skating hip.

Skater's often struggle to hold edges because they lift their free *leg* but not their free *hip*. So many things can go wrong if hips aren't cooperating, so it's very important for skaters to develop an awareness of their hips and the difference between their hips being lifted versus dropped. Refer to chapter eight for more information about hip lift drills.

Edges Recap:

- Alternating edges are a foundation for every moves test going forward
- They are introduced in Basic Skills classes but mastered over time
- Lift free hip higher than skating hip on outside edge and level to skating hip on inside edge

*Spirals*

You know those experiences when you were a kid where you really messed up and you knew you messed up so it stuck with you for the rest of your life? That's what spirals are to me. When I was eleven, I was running my program and doing a backward spiral when, suddenly, I felt a huge *thunk* and stopped abruptly. Unfortunately, it wasn't the wall I ran into, but a young skater. She was just tall enough for my skate boot to run into her, and thankfully, not my blade. I knocked this little girl over and she got a concussion. I still shudder thinking about that incident.

Because of that experience, I have a very strong respect for backward spirals and tell every single skater I coach that story and warn them to be extra careful of anyone performing spirals and to be cautious and aware when they are skating spirals.

I love teaching spirals to skaters because spirals require full body control; the kind of control we hope to see in so many areas of skating. Spirals look and feel floppy and insecure until that control is maintained.

Skaters performing a spiral must have proper control of their hips, free leg, blade position, and upper body position to keep the spiral from crumbling. I often look at skaters' spirals to see how much body awareness they have as well as strength.

When performing a forward spiral, skaters should glide forward on the middle to back of the blade. To achieve this weight placement, skaters need to practice bending at the waist (purposefully aiming for a "breaking at the waist" position). You may have noticed skaters hold a spiral position at the wall and slowly glide backwards, away from the wall, until they roll to their toe picks. This is a result of not pressing their skating hip back far enough and their skating foot forward far enough. The boot should be beneath the skater's chest and the angle between the skater's body and skating leg should be acute; not ninety degrees.

The hip-forward and probable bent-knee position is often the position a skater holds in a moving spiral just before they hit their toe pick and fly forward into a superman pose – something we all have done and enjoy so much. To avoid this common mistake, skaters can practice the skating leg position on two feet first. This is an awkward position to stand in and I always wonder what spectators think when I demonstrate it because it isn't your typical, graceful skating pose.

The key while practicing this position is to have skaters slightly arch their lower back, keep their shoulders back, arms at shoulder level, head up, legs locked, and hips pressing backwards. Their skates should not be directly under their hips at this point, but under their navel or chest instead. This way, skaters glide with their weight balanced toward their heels.

Once skaters master the two-footed spiral position at a standstill, they can try to maintain that position while moving across the ice. Finally, they can attempt the position on one foot. Spirals should be practiced at home, on the wall at the rink, and moving. Some skaters will struggle more with strength and some with flexibility, but both areas need to be focused on in order to improve their existing spirals.

The spiral pattern in Pre-Preliminary adds extra difficulty to spirals because skaters must be able to hold each spiral ½ the length of the rink and switch from one spiral to the next with only one push. The push is like the alternating forward outside edge pushes on the line.

Spirals Recap:

- The weight in forward spirals should be in the middle to back of the blade
- Skaters should lock both legs and press their hips back
- Skaters should feel the free leg's glute and leg engaged and turned out
- Spirals should be practiced on and off the ice

*The Waltz 8*

The Waltz 8 is made of three simple steps, but they are difficult to execute correctly. At the pre-preliminary level, skaters will naturally struggle with the right amount of edge control and timing, which makes it one of the most challenging patterns to master. I begin teaching this pattern to skaters early because it is difficult, and mastery takes time. By the time a skater makes it to Free Skate 2, they have been given all the tools to execute the circle 8: they learned forward three-turns, back outside edges, and the backward outside mohawk from Pre-Free Skate. I begin introducing the pattern in small pieces at this point in time.

Breaking this pattern into mini goals helps skaters to slowly progress in the pattern over time, without becoming too frustrated early on. The waltz 8 is a waltz and, therefore everything is set to a count of 6. Each third of the circle is a 6-count, to be more specific. The first three-turn is performed on a 6 count, as is the back outside edge and the forward outside edge. Skaters can demonstrate their ability to maintain the rhythm of the pattern, based on how they time out each step. I usually give them a week to work on the three-turn first, because, as simple as a three-turn may seem, they need to be very controlled, turn at the right timing, and make sure it will fit the pattern.

First, skaters can perform their forward outside three-turns in both directions on a hockey circle. From there, skaters should push off from a standstill, count to three, then turn and check their shoulders as they turn. Lastly, have them hold a back inside edge for a count of three. Breaking the pattern up into pieces helps skaters focus on getting each step/turn strong before putting it all together. Once they can hold the edges properly with the correct timing, the pattern usually just fits, and skaters are able to make the figure eight out of their steps. I usually have skaters start the pattern on their strong side so that they have some speed by the time that they get to the weaker side.

To hold the back outside edge without sub-curving into the circle is usually the most difficult part of the three-turn for skaters. Keeping their free hip level will help prevent a sub-curve. Also, it helps skaters to keep their heads still as they turn. During the turn, only their hips turn under them, and their shoulders rotate the opposite way, but their heads remain still. Heads weigh quite a bit and can shift a skater's balance on an edge, and inner ears help to maintain balance as well, so, during turns, when a skater's head remains still and continues looking in the direction of travel, the skater will perform a more controlled turn.

54

Once skaters accomplish the three-turn with the timing in both directions, they can add the back outside edge to it. The edge in this pattern is like the back outside edge in the alternating edge pattern's push but the lobe is not as sharply curved. Therefore, when skaters practice it, they need to be sure to push down hard on the push with a strong ankle bend and transfer their weight quickly to the skating foot. They can extend their free foot in front of them, locked, pointed, and in line with the skating foot. Their shoulders and arms need to be rotated over the circle, with their head looking into the direction of travel.

Skaters hold this position for three counts and then slide their free foot along their skating foot and let it pass to their ankle for the remaining three counts. At this time, skaters need to keep their hip lifted and body leaning into the circle. (Skaters can also lock and extend their free leg behind them for this part). I find skaters have more control when they keep their free leg tucked beside them, but it looks aesthetically pleasing to extend their free leg and point it if they can maintain control during the process.

The final, and most difficult step to this pattern is simply the back outside c-step (mohawk) which is the step from the back outside edge to forward outside edge (this step is defined as a c-step because it is a step which changes directions and remains on the same edge the whole time). Controlled shoulder rotation that rotates counter to the circle is crucial before, during, and after this step. Skaters can rotate their shoulders and turn their head to look outside of the circle on the 5 or 6 count of the back outside edge.

For example, when traveling on a left back outside edge, they would rotate their shoulders to the right and turn their head from looking over the left shoulder to the right shoulder. On the right back outside edge, this would be the opposite. I have found that skaters have a difficult time remaining on the back outside edge for the full six count before stepping forward onto the forward outside edge. A lifted hip, tight core, and head looking in the direction of travel can work wonders on a skater's ability to hold a back outside edge.

As skaters' step onto the forward outside edge, they must strongly check their shoulders and keep their shoulders strongly rotated outside of the circle in which they are traveling. Often, I place my hand on the skater's back shoulder blade and have them continue to press into my hand as they hold their edge and return to the center of the waltz 8. If a skater glides on a right back outside edge, I would have my hand against their left shoulder blade when they are rotated out of the circle and ready to step. Then, while the skater steps forward onto a left forward outside edge, I quickly move my hand to the right shoulder blade so that they can push that shoulder back quickly against my hand as they step.

Skaters can keep their free legs tucked, free hip lifted, and continue to glide toward the center.

*Forward Crossovers*

Forward crossovers use two major sources of power: the first source is the first push in a crossover, which resembles a stroke or chasse (see the chasse section of ice dance in chapter seven for more information on chasses). The second source is the second push in a crossover which is the most difficult portion of the crossover. Most skaters miss that part and just lift their legs up and over when performing crossovers, but there is so much more to them than crossing feet. Skaters also maintain power during crossovers by pushing down into the ice and leaning on their edges.

Technically speaking, crossovers are misnamed. They should be called cross-unders. Crossovers that are performed correctly do not cross the front foot *over:* the back foot crosses *under* the front foot instead. This is a crucial piece of information for those who want to gain power from that second push in the crossover. The skating foot should bend and push on an outside edge and push under the front foot. When skaters just start out, they may begin by crossing one foot over the other to get used to the weight transition, but they should work toward skating cross-unders as soon as possible.

During crossovers, skaters move in a circle or on a lobe and they should have their upper body rotated into their circle as well as their blades leaning on edges into the circle. The hips remain tucked, and ankles bend as much as possible during the crossover. Skaters need to carry out the crossover as though they are traveling through a low cave and if they rise up they will bump their head on the cave's ceiling. As skaters get more advanced in crossovers, they should lilt during the crossover (the skater rises up for a moment on the first and second push in order to add power to their skating leg).

*Isolate Each Crossover Push*

Isolating the two pushes in a crossover can greatly benefit the quality of the crossovers, especially since the first push tends to get sloppy and the second push is often non-existent in a crossover. The first push can be worked on as a chasse on the circle. Skaters absolutely love to push their feet straight back, using their toe pick on this inside edge push and causing all coaches, everywhere, to cringe.

The second push in the crossover is the most difficult. Skaters usually don't encounter a push with the outside edge until they begin crossovers. The push takes practice for skaters to grow accustomed to it. Skaters sometimes roll their ankles on this push, causing the boot to drop down toward the ice. They should be sure to keep their ankles in line with their knees and hips, in a straight line but on a slant, to avoid this error. Skaters can improve this difficult push by isolating it in the crossover: have skaters perform a pump with the outside foot while keeping both blades on the ice and then cross the back foot under and extend it. They can focus on the blade pressure and the ankle bend while working on this push.

57

*The Clock*

One effective way to explain to skaters where their free leg should go during a crossover or stroking push is to use the clock analogy or the 45-degree angle analogy (I like to remind skaters to have their teachers thank me someday since I teach them geometry, math, and physics on the ice all the time).

The clock analogy goes like this: skaters face the wall and hold it with both hands. Tell them the wall is 12 o'clock which means that directly behind them is 6 o'clock. Have the skater open their right foot so that it makes a "v-position" with their back foot. A "t-position" would mean the skater is pointing to 9 o'clock or 3 o'clock, but, with the v-position, we are aiming for the toe to point to 2 o'clock or 10 o'clock, depending on the foot. As they extend this back foot, following in the direction of the "v," skaters should reach their free foot back to 4 or 5 o'clock (right foot) or 7 or 8 o'clock (left foot).

*45-Degree Angle*

A second way to describe this same concept is in terms of geometry and having a skater's free leg reach back to a 45-degree angle. Describe, or better yet, draw, a 90 degree in which the first ray of the angle stretches parallel to the boards and the second ray stretches directly away from the boards, or perpendicular to the boards. Between those two rays, there is the ray that would intersect it, directly through the center. This is the 45-degree angle and it's the line that the free leg should follow when extended. Their free leg should never extend straight back to the 90-degree angle mark, but should go in between the right angle and extend toward the corners of the rink when facing the boards along the long axis of the rink.

Skaters will feel their entire leg engaged while holding this position: from their hip to their pointed toes. They should really squeeze their glute muscles and feel like someone is pulling on their blade the whole time (in other words, their leg is stretching long from their body). The more skaters hold this position at the wall and off the ice, the better the position will be while moving and also focusing on balance. Coaches can push down on the free leg boot and see if skaters can hold it still and not let it drop. I constantly remind skaters that skating isn't comfortable and, if they are overly comfortable in any position, it is probably incorrect.

Forward Crossovers Recap:

- Skaters should isolate each of the two pushes in a crossover to be sure they can achieve power from both
- The free leg position takes a lot of training and skaters should practice it on the wall and off the ice
- Skaters should lean into the circle and rotate their upper body into the circle

*Backward Crossovers*

Toe scratching: This is what comes to mind when I think of coaching backward crossovers and I'm sure most coaches would agree. Skaters forget to bend, and they also like to lean forward during these which results in the nails-on-the-chalkboard sound that we all love so much. The best way to avoid scratchy backward crossovers is to work hard on non-scratchy backward pumps.

A skater's weight should be in the middle-front of the blade during backward skating. That means they should feel as though they are standing with their head over their arch as they skate, and it may tilt more toward the front of the arch (just behind the ball of the foot). You will hear a skater's toe picks if the skater's nose goes over the toes. Instead, skaters should bend their ankles a lot and skate backward with the feeling that someone is pulling their hair or ponytail along behind them as they skate.

The best way to improve new backward crossovers is by practicing backward pumps. A lot of skaters will pump backwards by drawing a half circle with their outside foot and pulling the pumping foot close to the leaning foot so that the skater's heels meet. This is incorrect and makes backward crossovers very difficult. The feet cannot cross effectively if the heels of both feet are next to one another. Instead, the pumping foot should push out in front of the leaning foot and lock without any weight on it. Skaters can test that their pumping foot locks without weight on it by fully extending their pump and then lifting the leg to make sure that it is light and can lift. Basically, skaters should feel as though they are pushing their pumping leg away from them and leaving it out in front every time, they pump rather than pulling it back to the leaning foot.

For skaters to return their pumping foot to their side, they should simply rise in their knees and allow the pumping foot to return naturally, while the weight remains over the foot that is leaning into the circle on an outside edge. This prevents skaters from pulling their pumping foot around and drawing a half circle on the ice, resulting in the heels of both boots meeting. That motion will not create much power but will cause a lot of toe scratching on the ice.

There is an important weight transfer that occurs during the pump. Let's use clockwise backward pumps as an example (in this direction, skaters pump with the right foot and lean on an outside edge into the circle with the left foot). At the beginning of the push, the right foot will be turned slightly inward, toward the left foot and the right ankle will be bent with a significant amount of weight on it. Skaters push into the ice with the right foot on the inside edge and will then stretch the right leg out, away from their right leg, as they move backward. As the right leg straightens during the pump, the weight will be transferred onto the left side (at this point skaters should be able to lift their right leg in the air because there is little to no weight on it).

*The Inside Edge Foot During the Cross*

Next, skaters push onto their left outside edge and cross that foot under the right foot. As their left foot passes behind the right foot, the weight should transition onto the right back inside edge again.

Skaters often make the mistake of pulling their right foot toward them at this point (see the information about a proper backward pump) and this results in the toe pick of the right foot sitting directly beneath the nose. Whenever a skater's nose is directly over their toes and they're in a bent knee position, you will hear the scratching like nails on a chalkboard.

*The Outside Edge Foot During the Cross*

The outside edge foot contains all the skater's weight on it as the second (outside edge) push of the crossover begins. The skater should feel the outside edge cutting into the ice as they push the foot beneath them and extend their leg to a locked position. The bent ankle and knee transitioning quickly into a locked knee and pointed left toe is the power source of this push. Skaters will gain speed the harder they push and the faster their ankle explodes from flexed to pointed.

As the blade leaves the ice, the weight on the blade rolls forward from the middle of the blade all the way to the very bottom toe pick. This toe pick may hit lightly as the skater points the toe, but it is not the same as an actual toe push. A toe push occurs when a skater doesn't bend enough and just pushes their foot backward off of the toe instead of using the blade for the push.

Backward Crossovers Recap:

- The best way to improve backward crossovers is by practicing backward pumps using the correct push, posture, and lean

- The weight should be in the middle-front of the blade during backward skating
- Skaters should cross their back (outside edge) foot *under* the front (inside edge) foot

*Mohawks or C-Steps*

Mohawks (recently renamed c-steps) are steps that turn a skater from one direction to the other (forward to backward or backward to forward). Skaters remain on the same edge during both steps in the c-step (either both inside or both outside). Like three-turns, skaters have one side that they favor (the one that turns in the direction that they spin) and one side that is more difficult. There are several different c-steps but let's focus on the two most skated c-steps: the forward inside c-step and the backward outside c-step.

*Forward Inside C-Steps*

The forward inside c-step begins gliding on a forward inside edge and ends gliding backward on a backward inside edge. Skaters must open their hips to c-step properly. They should also have their shoulders rotated strongly into the lobe they are skating, over the free side. For example, when performing a right forward inside c-step, skaters should rotate their shoulders over their left (free) side when they glide forward on their right inside edge. Then, as skaters step backward onto the back inside edge, they should quickly and strongly rotate their shoulders so that they are still facing into their circle and are now strongly rotated over the right (free) side.

Some skaters struggle with opening their free hip enough to step down backward on a lobe and often step forward accidentally. Skaters can hold the position their free leg should be in right before they step either at the wall or while moving, to help with the turn out. When skaters c-step, the heel of their free foot should touch the arch of the skating foot. They should practice skating on a lobe with the free foot heel touching the skating side arch the whole time. The toe of the free foot should also be facing

62

away from the skating toe, so that the hips are very open. The free leg should be bent, and the ankle flexed.

Once a skater can hold a forward inside edge with their shoulders rotated over their free side and their free leg bent, flexed, and rotated open, they can begin practicing stepping down onto the free foot to create a back inside edge. Several things must happen when skaters step onto the back inside edge. They need to quickly check their shoulders in the opposite direction to keep control. Skaters should also practice c-steps without turning their head. When they begin the c-step, they should be looking forward in the direction of travel. When they step down backward, they should continue looking over the same shoulder, in the direction of travel.

An important weight shift occurs during a c-step. Skaters begin by gliding forward on one foot and then shift all of their weight onto the other foot quickly. This step should be done very close and beneath the hips so that a skater's upper body doesn't move during the step (other than rotating during the shoulder check). A common error that skaters have during c-steps is lurching forward and breaking at the waist.

When skaters step during the c-step, the skating foot becomes the free foot, and its function is important for the remainder of the lobe. Skaters should feel the foot they were gliding on stretch straight behind them (there should be a straight line from the skating heel to the free heel). The free leg locks, turns out, and the toe points. Skaters should basically feel as though they are being pulled along by their free leg and it is stretching long behind them. Skaters often have their free leg swing into the lobe which causes them to lose control of the back inside edge.

There are a few focus points skaters should keep in mind while performing c-steps. The free hip during both parts of the c-step remains level with the skating hip so that the weight is evenly placed over the skating side. Also, skaters should keep their skating

63

ankle bent and they should be leaning into the circle throughout the entire step.

*Back Outside C-Step*

The back outside c-step also needs to be executed with an open free hip to be done correctly. Skaters first test this element in the waltz 8 during the pre-preliminary or pre-bronze test. Before skaters step, they should practice gliding on a back outside edge with their shoulders rotated counter to the circle and head looking back, in the direction of travel. Opening the shoulders will help the free hip to also open.

When skaters can balance themselves on an edge while gliding backward with their head and shoulders rotated, they can start practicing opening their free hip. It's helpful to keep the free foot firmly planted against the ankle part of the skating boot. Skaters can rotate the knee and hip so that the leg makes a "4" and the free knee is facing directly behind the skater (beneath the back arm). When the free leg remains against the skating leg and just rotates open, skaters can then step down and have a close and controlled step. This step prevents the upper body from lurching forward.

Just like with all c-steps and turns, the shoulders need to check strongly during the turn. I often rest my hand against a skater's back shoulder blade while they glide on the back outside edge and have them lean back and press into my hand. If skaters fail to check immediately and continuously, the upper body rotation causes them to lose control of the edge.

The second portion of the c-step occurs when skaters glide forward on this new outside edge. They need to maintain bent ankles and lean back so that they are gliding on the middle-back of the blade. Skaters should also continue to lean into their circle and keep their free hip lifted over the skating hip, so that they can remain on a strong outside edge.

64

C-Steps Recap:

- Skaters must open their hips to c-step properly
- The free hip during both parts of the c-step remains level with the skating hip so that the weight is evenly placed over the skating side
- The step should be done very close and beneath the hips so that a skater's upper body doesn't move during the step

# CHAPTER V

## THE SCIENCE OF JUMPING

Jumps have never been my favorite as a skater. I love coaching jumps and I absolutely love watching jumps but jumping itself was just not my thing when I skated. If you ask most skaters to choose, skaters almost always have a strong preference for either spinning or jumping and I am in the spinning group. I landed all of my doubles through double lutz but I spent most of my time on the ice spinning or working on edges and moves and definitely had to talk myself into practicing jumps every day.

As a coach, I am fascinated by diving further into the world of jumps because they are so technical, detailed, and satisfying. Spin mastery tends to happen more gradually, but, with jumps, a skater usually has that one, invigorating moment to celebrate, when they finally land a jump, they've been working toward and it's so exciting to experience.

There are so many fun jump drills that skaters can work on for their jumps and the possibilities for combinations and drills are only limited to the skater and coaches' creativity. In this chapter, I'll share some of the drills that have worked well for skaters and some information about each of the jumps that I've learned that make coaching them more straightforward.

*Two-Foot Turns & Swizzles*

Believe it or not, jump training begins with two-foot turns and swizzles. Two-foot turns introduce shoulder checking and rotation of shoulders against hips. Swizzles teach skaters ankle and knee bend as well as internal and external rotation of the hips. The

science behind jump technique is consistent throughout skating –
whether it is a waltz jump or a double lutz.

Skaters begin working on jumps on day with the Two-foot
hop. Two-foot hops train skaters to lift off the ice by bending ankles
to load the muscles then straightening their legs and pointing their
toes to explode off the ankles and gain height. At this point in time,
skaters discover that we straighten our legs to jump and the faster
and stronger we do this, the higher we rise in the air. During these
hops, skaters also practice keeping feet aligned with hips - a theme
skaters will have in all their jumps.

*Jump Direction*

The direction in which a skater naturally jumps, and spins is
not decided based on which hand they dominantly write with, as
many people have said over the years. I am left-handed and am a
"righty" skater and my co-coach for years was right-handed and
skated as a "lefty." I haven't seen a lot of correlation between the
hand skaters write with and the direction in which they rotate. Just
because most people are right-handed, and most people rotate
counterclockwise does not mean that the two correlate. I generally
do not ask skaters which hand they write with so that I'm not biased
while watching them skate. I prefer to look for their natural
rotational direction instead.

One interesting thing I've learned is that skaters will start
showing you their natural direction in the beginning, even in Basic
1 and 2. Skaters have a direction that feels more natural with most
things they learn, and it usually gives coaches a good idea as to
which way they will rotate in the future.

There are a few useful tests I like to have skaters perform
when trying to decide whether they jump clockwise or
counterclockwise. The first is to ask a skater to do a two-foot turn
or three-turn and take note of the direction they begin with first as
well as the direction that looks more natural (they will most likely

67

start with the side that they prefer). One direction will be more of a struggle, and they will often rotate their shoulders less on their weaker side. Another test is to ask the skater to hop and turn 45 degrees repeatedly in a circle and notice which direction they rotate (this can be performed on or off the ice).

A third test is to have skaters hop on two feet and then land on one – have them try this three times and note if they land on the same foot each time – generally the skater should land on their dominant side which will be their landing leg. If a skater lands on the left, he or she will be more likely to be a clockwise jumper and it is the opposite for landing on the right side (if the other tests prove this to be true as well).

Finally, the simplest test of all is to ask a skater to skate away from you and then turn back toward you and skate back - usually they will turn the way in which feels most natural, which could very well be their natural rotational direction. Skaters can also demonstrate their pivots for you so you can see which direction rotates more smoothly.

Another thing to keep in mind is that you can always ask a skater which way *feels* most natural. I recommend using all these tests before making a decision. Some skaters just aren't as obvious as to which way they prefer. I have coached a lot of lefty skaters, but since most skaters are righty, I tend to take extra time evaluating someone who is showing me they may be a lefty just in case, since the odds of being a lefty are stacked against them. I would estimate that 1 out of every 5 skaters I coach is a lefty skater.

Jump Direction Recap:

- Jump direction is not based on which hand a skater writes with
- Skaters will often show you which direction they rotate the most naturally early on in skating
- Use a variety of tests to determine jump direction

## Landing Positions

Skaters hold landing positions out of every jump and spin as well as during other positions on the ice such as waltz-threes and during moves patterns. Therefore, they matter. A lot. Just like so many other ice positions, skaters can practice these off the ice and on the boards. Skaters need to have their shoulders rotated over their skating hips for this position, so I usually have them face the boards with both hands on the boards and then rotate their hips underneath them (in either direction) but keep their shoulders facing the boards. This trick automatically puts skaters into a checked position in which their shoulders are rolled open and their chest is over their skating side.

Next, skaters can keep their backs straight, and drop into a nice ankle, knee, and gently hip bend. Finally, skaters will lift their leg, open their free hip, and point their toe. The free leg should be lengthened, locked, and squeezed so that there is enough pressure on it that they could keep their leg up even if someone pushed down on it.

When skaters have mastered the position on the wall, they can try it moving backwards on an outside edge. Generally, skaters will struggle to keep their upper body checked over their skating side while gliding on the edge. This problem occurs because their bodies are rotating in a circle, so their upper body naturally follows suit and rotates too. It takes a lot of practice and awareness to maintain the proper counter rotation in the upper body while gliding. One way that skaters can improve their checked position is by using props such as a hula hoop, cord, or hockey stick that they can hold rotated over their skating side. This brings awareness to the upper body so that skaters will notice when it starts rotating.

Landing-Position Recap:

- Skaters' shoulders should rotate over the skating hip
- Skaters' free legs should be locked and rotated open, and their toes should be pointed
- Skaters struggle to keep their upper bodies checked in landing positions and can use props to assist in keeping their shoulders rotated

## *h-position*

An h-position is the air position that skaters perform in jumps. In a proper h-position, a skater will lift the free hip and turn it inward. A skater's toe and knee should be turned inward as well. If skaters leave their free hip open in the h-position, it causes a wrap in their doubles and triples.

Skaters can practice h-positions on the wall and while gliding to train their bodies on their air position. They should engage their core and stand on a straight leg, practicing good posture and balance. This is a difficult position to achieve when skaters start working on it but it's important.

Skaters can practice the h-position with their shoulders checked over their skating hip. That means that if they glide on their right leg, the left shoulder is in front and the right shoulder is behind with their chest rotated directly over their right leg. Their left leg should be turned inward towards their right leg.

One way skaters can improve the internally rotated free leg position is by performing a swizzle position on the ice where both toes touch. Then they should lift one leg and hip up, bend their knee, and maintain the same internally rotated position in the air as their foot was in the swizzle. Basically, an h-position is a swizzle position in the air. Remember when I saw that everything on the ice had to do with swizzles? It's true!

Skaters can also practice their h-position on the boards. They face their body to the left if they are on the right leg and have their shoulders face the wall, over the right hip. That way, when they lift their left foot and internally rotate it, their toe will touch the wall. This helps skaters to really understand and feel the internal rotation of the h-position.

h-position Recap:

- An h-position is the air position skaters should achieve in their jumps
- Skaters should have their free side rotated internally
- Skaters should have their shoulders checked over their skating side during an h-position

*Waltz Jump*

Waltz jumps are a skater's first true jump. We know that they are simple to attempt and land with bad form because of the public session skaters who attempt them while flailing through the air, causing coaches and skaters to have heart palpitations. Argh. Skaters can perform waltz jumps incorrectly, but it's mastering all of the finite details of the jump that truly matters.

Sometimes the walk-through is more difficult than the jump itself and it's important that skaters master the walk-through in order to maintain control and recognize what goes on throughout the jump. A waltz jump is a change of axis jump that takes off forward and lands backward. When walked through on the ice, a waltz jump is a forward outside edge c-step.

While working on waltz jumps, skaters can practice checking, changing their axis, proper landing position form, h-position form, head placement, and more. To get height on a waltz jump, skaters should practice locking their knees and pointing their toes on take-off. The take-off feels as though they are pushing the ice away from them with all their strength to lift up.

71

During a waltz jump take-off, the arms and legs pass through as one. The arms and legs sometimes try to lift at different times, so it helps to think of them as connected so they move as one. Skaters can imagine they are connected through a string like a puppet and, if their arms move, their free leg moves with them at the same time.

Skaters will jump higher when they understand the concept of how to gain height when taking off from the ice. The skater bends first to load the muscles, then quickly springs off their knee and ankles by locking them and pointing quickly. The harder and quicker they explode off their ankles, the higher the jump will be. Skaters practice firing muscles quickly from flexed to pointed and locked, both on the ice and off the ice, by performing two foot and one-foot hops. Practicing those motions helps to increase jump height over time (it's also important to do off-ice training to strengthen the muscles used for jumping).

During the waltz jump, the shoulders must be paid close attention to prevent the jump from being swingy and out of control. If a skater takes off on the left foot to rotate counterclockwise, he or she should have the shoulders rotated to the right on take-off. In the air, skaters feel their hips rotate beneath them in a counterclockwise direction and their shoulders rotate to the right side in a clockwise direction.

To understand the shoulder check and hip rotation in the air, skaters can stand on two feet and perform a two-foot hop in which they rotate their hips and land facing the opposite direction. Skaters rotate their shoulders in the other direction to practice checking. This drill can also be performed skating forward.

The free leg and hip pass through in an h-position as they take off. In the air, skaters' weight switches to the other leg and they switch to the opposite h-position. Skaters should turn their hips under them and feel themselves switch their weight onto the other hip at the highest peak of the jump to perform the jump correctly.

When a skater lands a waltz jump, their shoulders are rotated over their right hip, their head also looks to the right to help control the rotation and their arms should open wide in a T-position. (For more information on this, refer to *checking* in the basic skills chapter) Skaters often confuse checking with turning their arms so that they make an "L" and are facing their right side. Checking refers to the upper body, not arms.

Waltz-Jump Recap:

- Skaters should be able to master a waltz jump walk-through with proper form and h-position
- A waltz jump is an outside edge mohawk in the air in which a skater changes axis at the top
- The arms and free leg pass through together on take-off
- Skaters check their shoulders during the jump and land with shoulders counter-rotated over their skating hip

*Toe Loop*

Toe loops are challenging for skaters because of the take-off edge, so skaters need to drill the take-off edge often. Once the skater lifts off in a toe loop, it is executed similarly to a waltz jump. Skaters can commonly get into the back outside edge for the toe loop from either a forward inside three-turn, a forward outside three-turn and step onto the edge, or a forward inside c-step and step onto the outside edge from the step.

Regardless of how they get there, it's important that skaters check their shoulders and bend their skating knee, ankle, and hip as they reach back with their free leg to pick. Skaters should enter a position here that I call the *power angle*, in which they are in a straight line from their head to their toe pick, but that straight line is slightly tilted forward at an angle.

73

When skaters pick, they should pick very lightly. Their toe is going to lightly pivot as they push off the ice. Their energy should not slam down into the ice from a heavy pick, but it should be directed upward instead. The skater's toe pick reaches behind the skating side hip and shoulder so that everything is lined up. Some skaters struggle with bending their leg when they reach, causing the leg to circle around too far to the side and their axis to lean on take-off. It's important that they straighten and stretch it behind them. This is something skaters will especially have to practice for combination jumps involving toe loops.

A lot of skaters will do a toe waltz instead of a toe loop. A toe waltz happens when skaters put their toe pick into the ice and just simply turn and waltz jump off the toe instead of going through the motions of a true toe loop. A true toe loop contains an outside edge draw, and the skaters lift off the heel of their edge foot as they transfer their weight to the picking foot on take-off.

The edge before the turn going into the toe loop is usually shorter and the edge after the turn (the back outside take-off edge) is usually slightly longer. The edge won't be overly curved, but it will curve slightly since it's an edge. Overly swingy entrances can cause jumps that aren't controlled.

Skaters take-off for their toe loops with locked legs and land similarly to waltz jumps. Some skaters practice toe-loops in which they take-off into an h-position with the free foot (similarly to salchow and waltz jump). I personally prefer having skaters lock their edge leg as they lift so that they gain extra height. This is one of those preferences that is up to each coach and may work differently for each skater.

Toe Loop Recap:

- Skaters should pick lightly, pivot on the toe, and take off from a back outside edge

- Skaters can go into toe loops several different ways, but they should be sure to check their shoulders and reach in the power angle position to take-off

*Salchow*

Salchows feel like waltz jumps in the air. They take off from back inside edges, which skaters usually get to from a forward outside three turn or a forward inside c-step.

Salchows tend to become very swingy, which means skaters need to practice checking their shoulders *during* the turn or step (that usually translates to turn and *then* check, but then it's too late and the control is lost).

As skaters begin to take-off the ice, they need to make sure their front shoulder doesn't swing ahead of them. Skaters need to spend a lot of time gliding in the back inside edge and remaining checked. Sometimes, I'll have skaters play a game where I have them hold a controlled back inside edge until I say "jump!" Once I say that, they have to perform the salchow as quickly as they can, from the back inside edge they are holding. It's a fun way for them to practice staying in the back inside edge with control. They also must figure out how to bend their ankle and tighten their edge for lift off once it's time to jump.

Using an appropriate salchow timing is necessary to prevent a swingy jump or a jump that is difficult to rotate. There are all sorts of versions of the count I have heard from other skaters and coaches, and I'll give some examples of ones that have worked well for me: "one, turn, one, two, up." In that count, the skater is doing a forward outside three-turn for the jump entry. The skater pushes onto the forward outside edge on "one," turns on "turn," bends on "one," bends *more* on "two," and pushes off their toe on "up."

The same count can be used with other words. For example, I've heard people use, "I. Like. Seven. UP" where they use the same rhythm as the other count and take-off on "UP." It's important that coaches and skaters use a count that works well for them, while keeping in mind that the skater should bend extra on the last part of the take-off edge before jumping.

The free leg never crosses the midline during the salchow take-off. This is something that I see a lot with swingy salchows: skaters are on a back inside edge and they take their free leg and swing it around their body as they turn to take off. Instead, skaters should feel their skating foot begin to deepen its take-off edge and, as it rotates forward for lift off, the free leg should come through next to the skating foot and form an h-position as the skater lifts into the air and locks and points the skating leg. Skaters never cross their free leg across their body as they jump a waltz jump, so they shouldn't do that for salchows either.

After checking the three-turn, skaters' shoulders can be square to their hips as they turn forward to take-off, but the skater will then turn their hips under them in the air to rotate and the shoulders will be checked again as the skater returns to the ice (see the two-foot jump drill under *waltz jumps*).

The mark on the ice for a salchow take-off curves at the end as skaters deepen their knee bends and create a tighter edge. There is a flag at the end of it, showing the toe pick marks as skaters roll to their toes and push off the ice.

Once skaters are in the air, they will perform the same motion as a waltz jump. They should switch their hips and h-position their new free leg so that they will land in an h-position as well. This jump switches at the top and skaters should aim to practice that hip switch often and as quickly as they can to prepare them for double and triple salchows.

Salchow Recap:

- Salchows feel like waltz jumps in the air: skaters should switch to the other hip at the top of the jump
- Skaters should practice salchows with a controlled and checked take-off
- Skaters should never cross their free leg across their midsection during a salchow

*Loop*

Loops are difficult to learn, especially to do correctly. They take off from a difficult edge (back outside) and they are the first jump skaters learn where skaters do not switch axes in the air. They are one of those hurdles that skaters have to overcome, similar to the scratch spin, back spin, and those terrible back inside edges in Pre-Preliminary and Pre-Bronze.

Skaters are often able to master loop jumps more easily when they learn them from forward inside three turns. One of the hardest parts of loops is getting skaters onto the back outside edge and creating enough rotation that they can curve and take-off. The forward inside three-turn entrance helps skaters to kick start their rotation that they will need for take-off.

Skaters perform the forward inside three-turn similarly to how they enter a backspin: they turn their hips under them, shoulders rotate over the skating side, and they turn to face the free foot and end up in an h-position, with the weight on the outside edge of the skating foot. Skaters should maintain strong control during the turn.

A sloppy h-position will make it very difficult for skaters to jump, because the hip can pull skaters to an inside edge. Skaters need to feel as though their weight is balanced over a back outside edge and should be careful not to drop their shoulders, or any part of the upper body, into their circle. Holding their core strong during the three-turn assists with this.

Once skaters complete their forward inside three-turn, they deepen their ankle bend and roll to the front of their blade (roll hips forward and straighten) until they reach the toe pick and quickly lock and point their toe (jump). Skaters should complete this motion in one fluid movement so that they don't lose their momentum for the rotation. The take-off edge should look like a backward "j" for skaters who rotate counterclockwise. There will be a small flag at the end of the "j," which shows the toe mark and pivot on the ice.

By the time a skater takes off the ice in a loop, they are facing forward. The shoulders should not rotate ahead of them on take-off, but they can be square to the hips. In the air, skaters will rotate in an h-position and turn their hips under them 180 degrees so that they land backward and still in an h-position, with their shoulders rotated counter to their rotation direction and checked over their skating side.

The most difficult part of the loop is the take-off. Skaters can practice the outside edge take-off from the wall or gliding backward. The key is to have a controlled back outside edge that rolls all the way from the middle of the blade to the toe pick, while staying on the outside edge as the pressure increases and rocks forward.

Once skaters become comfortable with the take-off edge, they can work on the jump from the two-foot take-off position. During this position, skaters perform the exact same motion on the take off as they did from the three-turn entry, but they begin with their free foot on the ice, gliding in front of them. They initiate the turn with their ankle bend, edge pressure, and hip rotation, rather than just from the exit edge of the three-turn, which already sets them up for that curve.

It's important that skaters don't have their weight resting on the front foot. I like to think of that foot as more of a "training wheel" gliding along slightly in front of the skater so that they can lift it into an h-position without changing their weight placement. Skaters who struggle with putting too much of their weight forward, onto the front foot, can practice lifting that foot and setting it down without weight before take-off. As skaters lift off onto their toe pick, they should also drive their free leg up (the leg that was gliding in front) into an h-position. This motion, combined with the arms assisting on take-off, helps the jump gain height.

Sometimes skaters struggle with the air position, such as rotating in the h-position or checking their shoulders. One helpful drill is to glide forward slowly on two feet with their knees, ankles, and hips lined up in a two-foot glide position. Then, skaters can jump and rotate a half turn in their usual jump direction and practice turning their hips under them while rotating shoulders the other direction. They should land on one foot, gliding backward in an h-position with proper alignment over the skating side.

There are some differing opinions on arm positions during jumps, but the consensus seems to be that skaters should use them to assist in their take off. I prefer for skaters to use their back arm in a scooping motion (while being careful not to drop their shoulder) and to have their front arm pull inward in an open position (basically making a right angle and reaching toward the back hand so that they meet). This arm placement can be used across the board with all jumps. The only difference is in waltz jumps and axels, where skaters may have both elbows brush past their side and then lift up into the open-air position as the skaters take off.

Loop Recap:

- Skaters can learn loop jumps from forward inside three turns
- Skaters should practice control in their h-positions
- Skaters will deepen their knee and ankle bends as they roll to the front of the blade for take-off

- Skaters should keep their shoulders checked and use their arms for take-off

*Flip*

Flips are very similar to loops in the air but with a different take-off. Skaters remain on their take-off axis throughout the entire jump with their free leg held in an h-position. By the time skaters learn flips, they have usually mastered loops. Therefore, the air position, rotation, shoulder check, and landing of the flip will be familiar to skaters since they are the same as the loop. Skaters will just need to work on adding all those elements of the jump to the flip take-off.

Flips take off from the toe pick and a back inside edge. Skaters can enter flips many ways, but the two most common ways are from forward outside three-turns or forward inside c-steps. During their turn or step, skaters should bend and stretch so that there is an angle from their toe pick to the crown of their head. As skaters glide backward, they will transition their weight from the hip on the back inside edge to the hip of the toe pick foot. Skaters sometimes struggle lifting their free hip into the h-position as they lift because they don't transition their weight quickly enough. This is an important piece of the jump that can be practiced on its own while at a standstill or moving slowly.

The three-turn or c-step should be fairly straight (it will curve minimally since it is on an edge) and the first part of the turn or step should be on a shorter edge while the back inside edge can be slightly longer. Skaters need to feel control throughout their entire body as they reach their free leg back throughout the turn or step and then continue gliding backward as their weight shifts from the front foot to the back foot. When the skaters' picks reach the ice and they shift their weight over it, they will stand up and pivot on that toe until they find themselves facing the other direction. Skaters feel the standing leg locked and pointed and their hips pressed forward.

80

Some skaters struggle to stand fully over the locked leg and with their toe pick planted in the ice. They can practice this position by standing next to the wall on locked legs and shifting their weight forward so that their body slightly leans toward the wall and the hips are directly over the toes. This should feel like toe turns across the ice, where the skaters' toes are strongly planted into the ice rather than the bottom toe picks brushing the ice and the blade still slightly parallel to the ice.

Once skaters are familiar with this position, they can perform the three-turn or c-step followed by the reach and pick and rotate on their toe pick. It's very important that they rotate forward on their toe pick in an h-position, like how skaters take off for a loop.

As with all jumps, it's important that skaters lock the skating leg on the take-off to spring up and gain height. Once skaters can control the entry and shift from the back inside edge to the toe pick foot and do a pivot on that toe, they can jump the flip. The skaters jump into the air by pointing and springing off of their ankle and locking their leg as they lift their free leg into an h-position.

Skaters keep their take-off leg locked in the air and rotated inward and their free leg in an internally rotated h-position with their hip lifted. They turn their hips under them and keep shoulders checked over the skating side. After landing, skaters bend and send the free leg back into a strong landing position, keeping shoulders checked and their head looking into the direction of their circle (over their skating side).

Flip Recap:

- Skaters remain on their take-off axis throughout the entire jump with their free leg held in an h-position
- As skaters glide backward, they transition their weight from the hip on the back inside edge to the hip of the toe pick foot
- Skaters should be able to stand over their toe pick foot and pivot, in an h-position, with a locked leg

*Lutz*

Lutzes are related to loops and flips but with a different, often perceived as more challenging, take-off. Lutzes take-off from an outside edge. Skaters often tell me that they feel twisted and backward when they try to do a lutz jump because they feel their shoulders rotated one direction and then their body must turn and jump in the other direction. I tend to agree with them on this one and try not to overshare my all-around dislike of lutzes.

However, the same is true for a loop and a flip, it just feels different in a lutz because of the outside edge. Lutzes come more naturally for skaters if they focus on and train the outside edge take-off and then simply perform a loop jump once they're in the air.

I'll explain the lutz take-off by describing a lutz that rotates counterclockwise and takes off from the left back outside edge and right toe pick. Skaters glide backward on a back outside edge which becomes more active, with a deeper curve and more ankle bend, just before the skater shifts to the toe pick of the right foot for take-off. The curve of the back outside edge before take-off draws a backward "c" on the ice and it ends with a little flag that shows the skaters' weight transfer from the pinky toe of the left foot to the right toe pick.

The front of the left blade flicks the ice as it turns slightly on take-off. The blade of the left foot should *not* be in line with the right toe pick as a skater lifts off. When this happens, skaters stay on their left side too long and usually switch to an inside edge at the last minute, causing the skater to flutz (or do an accidental flip when aiming for a lutz). Instead, the left foot is very close to the right and internally rotated, but slightly in front of the right foot. The left foot lifts off the ice and into the h-position slightly before the right foot lifts because skaters will pivot forward on their right foot in the h-position as they take-off. This last portion of the outside edge and the transfer of weight to the right foot needs to be drilled and practiced repeatedly for a skater to feel the appropriate lutz take-off.

Skaters can practice the back outside edge on the wall by performing "outside edge swizzles" at the wall, which draw an hourglass figure on the ice. Skaters move their blades forward and backward, like swizzles, but they are on an outside edge and the blades will move parallel to one another in the middle of the swizzle and then move apart at the front and back. They have their heels facing each other and toes apart in front of them and then their toes facing each other and their heels apart at the back portion of the swizzle (they can scratch on their toe picks at this point since a true lutz does that on the outside edge). This drill helps skaters feel what happens on the back outside edge of the left foot, particularly how closely beneath the left hip the left foot will travel.

Once skaters master the outside edge swizzle drill on two feet, they can switch to skating the drill on just the left foot and then add the toe pick motion as well. Skaters will bend and reach a lot with the right foot to pick. As they get more comfortable drawing an outside edge and picking with the right foot, skaters can try the take off with a more scissor-like effect. This means they reach back with the right foot and are in the power angle as they glide on the active back outside edge, but by the time they pick, they speed up the back outside edge and rise in the skating knee and the right foot actually picks beneath the right hip. It looks like their legs are scissors opening as they reach but they close and draw together as the skater picks.

Skaters can work on the scissor motion on the wall, allowing their left toe to scratch, and then add the weight transfer and pivot to the drill later. Skaters scratch their left toe pick, and it turns inward and draws close (in front and slightly to the left) to the right foot. Skaters then stand up on their locked right foot with the toe pointed and pivot so that they are forward and face away from the wall, feeling all the weight on their right foot. When skaters become efficient in the left back outside edge and the transfer of weight and pivot on the right foot, they are ready to jump the lutz.

Skaters often struggle to keep their shoulders checked on the lutz take-off. They also struggle with maintaining a true back outside edge while they are moving. Skaters can practice the jump on the circle so that they can line up their shoulders over the circle, with the left shoulder in front and the right shoulder behind them. They can then practice a deep ankle bend as they reach and pick for take-off. The jump operates the same as the loop and flip, in which skaters remain over their right side, locked leg in a strong h-position, and turn their hips beneath them in the air. Skaters take off and land on the same foot.

Skaters can perform bad lutzes all day and think they are doing them correctly, but, when they train and focus on the back outside edge, they will find that a lutz is an incredibly difficult jump and takes lots of work and effort to get it right. Some skaters take just as long to land a true lutz as they do to land an axel.

Lutz Recap:

- Lutzes take-off from an outside edge and both toes are pointed inward during a lutz
- Skaters transfer their weight from the edge foot to the toe pick foot and should not pass the toe pick foot with the edge foot.
- The blade of the left foot should not be in line with the right toe pick as a skater lifts off
- Lutzes operate the same as the loop and flip, in which skaters remain over their right, locked leg in a strong h-position, and turn their hips beneath them in the air

*Axel*

Axels are a large hurdle to overcome for skaters as they are the first jumps that rotate over one rotation in the air, and they require more force and quickness in order to get them fully rotated. Skaters sometimes feel overwhelmed by axels. While they do take a lot of practice and time to master, by the time skaters begin axels, they have practiced all the parts that go into an axel and are ready to piece them together. For example, the waltz jump teaches skaters the axel take-off (which is why they should work on a controlled, checked walt take-off from the beginning) and the back spin teaches skaters the air position for an axel and the feeling of the rotation on the right side. An axel is also a waltz loop in the air, so it's important for skaters to have a controlled waltz loop.

There are so many drills and exercises skaters can practice to aid with axels. A lot goes into an axel in a short amount of time so it's very helpful for skaters to do lots of drills and lots of walk-throughs so that their bodies can just take over in the air and they don't have to overthink all aspects of the jump.

During a walk-through, skaters need to control their body movements and stay very aware of what their muscles feel like as they go through each step. Axels, like so many elements on the ice, eventually become something skaters just *feel* rather than think about so it's helpful for them to train their mind on focusing on the feeling of each part early on. For example, as skaters glide forward on their take-off edge, they feel their skating leg bent and their upper body strong and checked. As they press their hips forward and rock to the toe to take-off, they feel the skating leg locked and tight, as though the quad and calf are squeezing tight, and the toe pointed and pushing down. At the same time, they feel their core and hip engaged as they lift their free knee and hip and press them through.

When skaters walk-through axels like limp noodles, whipping their arms and legs around and not focused on where each part of their body is in space the whole time, they won't be able to land the jump. They can practice control by extending all parts of the jump in a walk-through so that they are forced to really feel what they are doing throughout. They can hold the forward outside edge with their free leg bent behind them, shoulders checked head forward, hips forward, and ankle bent for as long as possible before locking their right leg and sending their arms, and right knee, and hip through, into an h-position. Skaters hold the h-position if they can before turning their right hip beneath them and stepping down backward onto their right foot.

Skaters hold this air position on their right side if possible: right leg locked and squeezing, shoulders checked over the right hip, elbows squeezed in tight to the upper body on the right side, head slightly over the right side, left hip lifted, and ankles locked. There is so much that goes into that air position that skaters should train it often. Last, skaters can hold the checkout and landing positions. They lift their left leg and hip so that the left foot rises up the right leg and is ready to checkout (this position technically happens as skaters are just about to land).

Skaters then keep arms in tightly and kick the left leg back as hard as they can, like the feeling of a backspin checkout. In this position, a skater's head rotates into the circle over the checked shoulders and skating hip. The knee, ankle and hip are bent and lined up correctly. Skaters can practice axels with arms held in on the landing to prevent them from opening up in the air. Once skaters are comfortable with axels, they can transition to opening their arms upon landing.

In addition to walk-throughs, skaters should practice waltz back spins so that they can train the quick snap and rotation for the axel. The back spins pull in and rotate the second the skater's blade hits the ice. Skaters can also loop out of the back spin and then hold their landings (remember to keep arms in tightly).

There are lots of drills to work on a truly locked free leg and pointed toe for axel take-offs. Skaters can glide slowly at the wall on the left foot, then rock their hips forward, lock and point, and grab the wall to balance in that take-off position. Skaters really struggle with axel take-offs, especially when they fail to get their hips forward and bring the right hip through so that they can switch their axis quickly at the top of the jump.

86

Another common take-off struggle is a swinging axel. During a swinging axel, skaters pre-rotate their shoulders and take off from a very curvy forward outside edge, often swinging their right foot across their center axis. It's helpful to train controlled waltz and axel take-offs, in which skaters keep their right shoulder behind them on the forward outside edge. They can also use their head by looking at something (slightly higher, to help them jump up) but directly in front of them rather than to the left.

A skater should feel as though there is a wall beside them to the left as they take off. The right foot cannot rotate and kick through the wall but must go in front of the skater and rotate backward so that the skater continues the jump in a straight line in the air. They can practice this feeling by training the take-off position next to the actual wall: skaters face the wall, turn to their right to hold a small outside edge, bend and roll to the toe then hit the wall with their right foot and step down directly backward onto their right foot. They will keep the left hip lifted and quickly lock the ankles. At this point, skaters are facing to the left and their shoulders are directly over the wall on their right side.

Axels take serious mental and physical training. Skaters should visualize them, jump them off-ice, and drill them and jump them on ice. Even after skaters land axels, they need to continue drills to prevent axels from becoming swingy or sloppy.

Axel Recap:

- Axels are waltz loops in the air
- Skaters should walk-through axels, focusing on the feeling of all parts of the jump
- Skaters learning axels should keep their arms in on the landing to prevent opening in the air
- skaters should practice waltz back spins so that they can train the quick snap and rotation for the axel

# CHAPTER VI

## THE ART OF SPINNING

Spinning is complicated. Most skaters struggle to learn to find their center at first. There is, of course, a lot of science that goes into the ability to find their center and maintain momentum in a spin, but it is also an art that takes a bit of creative discovery since developing spins is different for every skater.

Teaching spins is like being in the Twilight Zone. There have been so many times where I have repeated the same concept over and over about an aspect of a spin and then, on the hundredth time, a skater looks at me and says, "Oh, you never said to do that before" as they finally perform it correctly. *Insert eyeroll here* Therefore, I explain the same concepts in as many different ways as I possibly can come up with and I draw the spins, tell stories, demonstrate them, have skaters walk through certain parts so they can feel the spin, and try to explain that they *need to straighten their leg* in every accent, dialect, and language I can think of.

Spins are frustrating to learn. Spins can be frustrating for coaches, too. But, with some useful tips and tricks as well as a deeper knowledge about what happens in spins, it doesn't have to be *face turning purple with rage* frustrating.

### All Spins Travel Backwards

Although there are countless variations of spins, there are technically only six basic positions that a skater can achieve; upright, sit, and camel, back upright, back sit, and back camel. The upright, sit, and camel are often called "forward spins" but it's important to note that there are no such things as forward spins (the exception is if one is referring to a change of edge spin variation). *All spins travel backwards.* "Forward" spins begin from a forward outside three-turn entry which puts skaters on a back inside edge while they are skating. They rotate backwards on these spins. Backspins also enter from a three turn and skaters also rotate backwards but skaters are on an outside edge instead of an inside edge for backspins.

*Upright Spins*

Skaters begin learning spins with 2-foot spins and these beginning spins are a great opportunity for skaters to learn about locking their legs, correct blade pressure into the ice, how to gain momentum and the proper body position in spins.

One of the most common challenges that new skaters face in achieving a balanced upright spin is to keep their knees locked in the spin. The goal is for skaters to balance their weight on the ball of the foot during the spin. Skaters sometimes bend their knees to rock forward rather than lock their knees and rock their hips forward. The bent knee position causes skaters to lose balance and travel.

Skaters can practice their locked leg position while standing still and while gliding backwards to train their body for when they are in the spin. The biggest thing for skaters to feel are their legs locked and hips rocked slightly forward (this should replace the ankle and knee bend they so often try to create). Also, to thoroughly understand what it means to have "locked knees" skaters should practice locking their knees while standing still and notice the difference between relaxed knees and locked knees.

A few things skaters will feel when their legs are locked are; their knees elongated and pressing backwards a bit, their quads will feel very tight and stiff, and their glutes will feel strong and engaged. Tightening their glutes while also locking their knees will improve balance even more since our glute muscles are a huge source of balance for our legs.

89

One challenge that skaters encounter with upright spins is the ability to produce enough momentum to initiate the spin. This begins with practicing pumps and being able to apply enough bend and pressure into the ice on a pump to start the spin (this should be similar when the skater is pumping during a pivot to start the spin or just a regular pump with both blades flat on the ice). Not only do skaters create power into the spin with their legs, but they can add arms to speed the spin up and keep their skating legs locked and pressing into the ice.

## Draw Half a Heart

The pattern in which we enter a spin has the most impact on the success of a spin. I have skaters begin learning spins on a line so that they can have a visual of where their spin should begin and where it should end. All spin entries should draw half a heart on the ice. Remember the days in school when you would fold a paper in half and draw half a heart in the center so that when you cut it out you had a full heart that was even on both sides? That's the exact pattern that a skater's blade draws on the ice - beginning at the line (think of it as the center of the paper) and ending back on that same line again but with a sharp hook at the top.

For skaters to draw this half heart shape, they must start on an outside edge and increase the depth of the edge as they glide so that the edge tightens and curves back to face where they started from on the line. This tight edge that three-turns is called the hook. The hook causes the spin to begin naturally and not feel forced. It is so important for the spin to begin naturally. Achieving the hook is the most difficult part of the spin entry and, when done incorrectly, it can be the reason a spin travels or does not spin at all.

There are several things that must happen during the entry edge for a skater to create a hook and properly enter a spin. First, the skater must increase ankle bend while holding the edge. The ankle and knee bend should be present as they push into the edge, but they should continually increase the bend as they grow closer to the hook until they feel a significant amount of ankle pressure against the front of the boot.

Second, a skater must increase their lean as they grow closer to the hook. A skater's lean increases with speed and ankle bend as the pressure into the ice increases, but it is crucial that they allow themselves to lean enough that they feel slightly off balance entering the spin. A cautious spin will be upright and stiff but a spin with a lot of lean and bend will create momentum and will become more balanced during the spin. Remember, from the section on edges, that this lean is initiated from the blade and the knee, ankle, and hip lean as one. Some skaters drop their shoulders into the circle on spin entries and it causes them to lose control.

Finally, a skater must rock forward on the blade while entering a spin. During the initial push off the line, the blade pressure should be towards the middle to back of the blade. As they near the hook of the spin, the skater rocks forward on the blade so much that they tap their bottom toe pick during the hook. The toe pick taps on the pinky toe side and then a skater will straighten up and stand on the inside edge of the blade while spinning. It's helpful to have skaters stand still on the ice and practice bending their ankles and rocking forward on their blades until they feel their bottom toe pick tap the ice, to achieve this while moving.

If you are brave enough and quick enough, it is possible to pull a skater into the hook by standing on the line with them, holding their front arm, and pulling them along, helping them to gain speed into the spin. Just be sure to move out of the way quickly as they enter the hook, or you will be kicked by the free leg. Although this movement is tricky to orchestrate, it can give skaters the correct timing sensation of the hook.

*Push Everything off the Table*

There are several other ways that skaters can add force to the spin in the beginning. One way is by using their shoulders and arms

91

to initiate momentum in the entrance. Some skaters start off with square shoulders and some rotated outside of the direction that the spin will travel, and some rotated into the spin. There are pros and cons to all beginning upper body positions, but I have had the most luck with skaters rotating their shoulders outside of their spin when they push into the entry edge. This allows skaters to then turn their torso strongly into the direction of the spin as they reach the hook of the spin with their blades, and it adds to their momentum.

The entry edge causes a skater to rotate in the direction of the edge, so it is very difficult to keep their shoulders rotated outside of the circle as they glide on the edge. This is something important to practice and I find it helps to have skaters imagine that their back arm and free leg are connected so that they stretch behind them through the entire spin entrance and do not rotate forward until slightly after the hook has been completed. You will notice when a skater brings their shoulders and free leg around too quickly in a spin because it will look like they are swinging into the spin and they are initiating the spin with their free leg momentum, but it causes a messy, traveling spin.

Skaters can really use their arms and keep their shoulders level by imagining that they are *pushing everything off a table* after they complete the hook in a spin. They can first practice this from a standstill in which they rotate their shoulders and arms away from the direction of the spin (to the right if they spin counterclockwise) and then quickly rotate their arms in the opposite direction until they are just past centered over the hips but slightly rotated to the left (have them imagine that their belly button stops over their left foot instead of centered between both feet). Some skaters push everything off the table very timidly, meaning they rotate too slowly with their arms, so it's a good idea to have them practice it from a standstill with arms locked and imagine they are angrily sending everything flying off the table.

## Crossing the Free Leg

After the hook, it's a good idea for skaters to hold the v-position for a few revolutions to center their spin before pulling in. It's preferable for legs to pull in first and arms to follow. However, skaters must remain still while legs and arms move. While skaters move their legs and arms, they should maintain focus on pressing down into the ice on the spin spot. The blade moves very easily during a spin and will lose its positioning the moment the skater stops pushing down. Skaters should press down with the part of their foot that is over the spin spot of the blade as though they are trying to drill a hole through the ice. The entire skating side should feel engaged.

The free foot crosses at the height of the skating knee. The skater brings the free foot in to rest against the outside of the skating leg while keeping the free leg and hip facing forward and trying not to externally rotate the free leg. The skater should keep the free hip up while crossing. As the skater presses the free leg down to cross at the ankles, the heel should remain flexed, and the free foot should rub against the skating leg as it lowers toward the ice. Skaters should push the free foot down with strength, as though they are pushing through mud, to keep up momentum in the spin.

While ankles are crossed, the free foot remains flexed so that the heel is parallel to the ice, but the toe is slightly pointing toward the ceiling. The legs and ankles should be close together as though they both have magnets attached to them and are pulled toward one another. As a spin speeds up, the ankles will naturally pull apart, so it is up to the skater to keep them locked together and remain spinning. Spins that have a gap between the free leg and skating leg are less controlled, slower, and look sloppier.

## Limp Noodle Arms

Most new skaters do not add very much to their spin while pulling arms in because they pull their arms in as though they are limp noodles rather than with strength. I help skaters drop noodle arms by directing them to make a circle with their arms in front of their body, as though they are holding a basket. Then I place hands on their wrists, or top of their arms *on the inside of the basket.* Skaters pull their arms in, and I pull their arms toward me, creating some tension that they have to overcome.

Once skaters have experienced this pressure, they can create that tension on their own. They hold the invisible basket again and, this time, pull their arms toward them while simultaneously pushing their arms out, creating the muscle tension that will aid the speed of their spins. Another way for skaters to create this pressure is to imagine that they are holding a balloon during a spin, and they need to squeeze their arms tightly enough to their chest so that they pop the balloon.

Upright Scratch Spin Recap:

- Skaters should lock their legs, squeeze their glutes, and rock their hips forward to achieve the correct upright position in a spin
- Skaters draw half a heart on the ice during the entrance and should deepen the ankle bend, increase their lean, and rock forward on the blade as they near the hook of the spin
- Skaters hold their free leg behind them during the spin entry and bring it forward after the hook of the spin
- Skaters cross the free foot at their skating knee and keep legs and ankles squeezing together throughout the spin
- Skaters practice using their arms from a standstill (pushing everything off the table)

*Upright Backspins*

After the struggle of learning a scratch spin and finally achieving balance on their spin spot, we have the privilege of informing skaters that there's an even *more* difficult spin to master: the backspin. (Side note: this is usually when I like to explain to skaters that the challenges in figure skating are never-ending and that is what makes the sport fun and worth continuing. If it was easy, anyone could do it). Skaters struggling through a backspin usually don't like hearing this, but I like to think the idea sinks in eventually.

There are many different drills to get skaters started on backspins. The drills are helpful because a different and difficult spin spot is required for the back spin. Like their scratch spins, skaters need to put pressure on the front of the blade, but the spin spot will be on the outside edge instead of the inside edge. When you picture how narrow a blade is, this is a very small difference of only about a centimeter but it's pivotal that skaters find the outside edge for these spins.

One key for skaters in mastering a backspin is understanding the mechanics of the backspin. Skaters travel backward on their blades during a backspin, which is why the pressure is on the front of the blade. The pressure will be on the spin spot which is just behind the toe pick and it's the spot where skaters will feel the least amount of friction on the blade. They can practice feeling this spin spot by locking their leg and pulling the foot backward so that the ball of the foot is directly beneath the hip on the ice (rather than the arch of the foot that is usually more naturally beneath the hip when standing).

Once skaters have their hips lined up over the spin spot, they can rock forward on the blade and press the front of their blade into the ice and gently twist it side to side as though they are squishing a bug. If skaters are on the correct part of the blade, they won't feel any scratchiness or create any snow. It will be very slick and turn easily. Practicing this motion is useful because it is hard to find this spot and maintain pressure on it during the spin.

When skaters begin the back spin, they rotate the skating hip under them so that it is strongly turned inward. Skaters can practice pumping in backward pivots with their back spin toe pick planted in the ice and turned inward. This is a great drill to practice because holding the hip internally rotated is tough and takes a lot of hip awareness and control. Skaters can also practice finding the spin spot by performing their regular two-foot spin (with the weight on the left ball of the foot and right heel for a skater who spins counter-clockwise). During the spin, skaters can internally rotate their right hip and press their weight onto the right front of the blade so that the right foot goes from spinning forward to spinning backward.

Once skaters are comfortable on the spin spot on two feet during a two-foot spin, they can try the two footed backspin and then lift their left foot briefly to see if they can hold their balance on the right outside edge for a moment or two. The key is to keep their free hip lifted into an h-position and keep their shoulders rotated over the right side.

Skaters learn the backspin from a pivot entrance and/or the three-turn entrance. The inside three-turn should lean deeply and create a half heart pattern, like the scratch spin, in which the skater holds the edge all the way back to the line before beginning the spin. When skaters hit the hook of the spin, they are extremely bent in their skating ankle with weight all the way forward on the blade so that the inside toe of the right foot taps the ice lightly. At this point, the skater should rotate their right hip inward to face the left leg that is either dragging or extended behind the skater, thus transitioning their weight from the inside edge to the outside edge of the blade.

Skaters struggle with the entry of this spin, so it helps to try breaking it down at the wall. They can stand very close to the wall on their right foot, rotated open so that it's beneath the right shoulder. Skaters should have their chest and shoulders facing the wall. The left toe should be lifted off the ice and stretched long (mimicking its position during the entry edge). The left toe should also be lightly touching the wall.

Skaters turn their right hip beneath them so that they face the left foot. The left foot should not leave the wall. The toe continues touching the wall and remains turned inward while the leg lifts into an internally rotated h-position. When skaters' hips turn beneath them, their shoulders should press strongly to the right and remain planted over the wall, while the lower half of their body is facing to the left. They will find themselves in their usual h-position. Keeping their left foot against the wall is very important, since a lot of skaters will enter their back spin and allow their left foot to rotate behind them instead of turning to face it. Turning directly toward the left foot and creating a strong backspin position is critical to beginning their backspin. This keeps skaters over their right sides.

Once skaters can enter the spin properly, they can practice increasing their speed by going from a controlled h-position to a tightly closed free leg. This part of the spin should operate similarly to the scratch spin, in which the skater crosses the free foot high at the knee and then tightly pushes the outside of the free ankle all the way down the side of their skating calf until the ankles are tight.

In a backspin, the toes of both feet can point toward each other. The arms can also pull in tightly. They should pull in from the right side, elbows first, tight against the upper body and the skater should squeeze the arms onto the right side of the body throughout the spin. The tension between the legs and upper body, combined with the pressure into the ice with the spin spot will generate extra momentum for the spin. Skaters need to remember to keep the free hip lifted so that their weight remains on the skating side.

Finally, as skaters begin to rotate their backspin on the front of the blade (they will spend a lot of time rocking to the heel or rotating forward on the back of the blade in the beginning), they can practice checking out. The checkout is more difficult than the scratch spin checkout because it operates less like a push onto a new foot and more like a backward power pull. Skaters can bend their ankles and press down into the ice while also lifting the crossed free leg. They should then open their arms and press onto the outside edge with the skating foot and rise in the knee so that they develop speed backward out of the spin. This should happen as the skater simultaneously kicks their free leg back into a landing position to generate added power.

Back Spin Recap:

- Skaters need to find the spin spot on the outside edge of their blades near the pinky toe
- Skaters can practice pivoting over their backspin toe while rotating backward and keeping their hip internally rotated
- Skaters should keep their free hip lifted into the h-position and keep their shoulders rotated over the skating side
- Skaters checkout of back spins with a power pull motion

*Sit Spins*

Sit spins are often easier for skaters to master than back spins. Skaters are introduced to the spins simply by reviewing a dip position. Skaters practice bending into a full dip as quickly as they can, noticing how they bend their ankles and knees a lot, and send their hips back as though they are sitting in a chair. Then they practice standing out of the dip by pressing their hips forward, pushing down with their feet, and squeezing their glutes.

Once skaters have practiced the sit position, which needs to be done very quickly as they enter the spin, they can practice their free leg position for the spin. They do this by holding the wall, rotating their body to the left or the right (left if they spin on their right foot and right if they spin on their left foot), and stretching their free leg behind them as though they are entering a scratch spin. Skaters then circle their free leg around, feeling as though someone is pulling on it and it is stretching their leg as far from their body as possible (to create momentum and keep it straight). As they bring their leg around, they will rotate their free hip so that their toe is facing away from them as they pull the free leg in front.

I usually take a skater's boot and move their leg for them the first time, to demonstrate this motion. As their free leg approaches their skating leg, they should feel like the free leg is being led by their heel, rather than their toes. The free leg remains locked and turned out and touches the skating leg just below the knee when the skating leg is bent. When the free leg approaches the skating leg after the hook in the spin entrance, skaters feel as though the free leg is being pulled magnetically toward the skating leg, to increase spin momentum. Also, if the free leg remains open and separated from the skating leg, the skater's weight pulls to the free side and the hip may drop, causing the skater to fall out of the spin.

Another way that skaters can practice their sit position, including the free leg, upper body, and arms, is by trying the position on a bench off the ice. This allows them to feel how far back their hips have to bend in order to feel like they are sitting. They can stretch their free leg in front of them and see how to hold it rotated open and parallel to the ground (when their free leg starts to tilt downward toward the ice too far in the spin, it prevents the skater from getting lower in their spin).

*Arms in a Sit Spin*

There are lots of arm variations in sit spins, but, when learning a sit spin, arms are straightforward and can be held in a locked position in front of the skater. I prefer skaters to enter the spin like they would a scratch spin; with their shoulders and arms rotated outside of the spin and, as they hit the hook, they *push everything off the table,* turning their shoulders and arms slightly more toward their skating side, but opening their arms wide and keeping their elbows locked. Skaters should bring arms together quickly as they sit and stack their hands one on top of the other, with thumbs tucked underneath, kind of like they are making a hand puppet.

A skater's arms can maintain some tension in the spin as well. I set my hands under their stacked hands and have them press down with their locked arms. This is what they should feel when they are in the spin because the force that their locked arms make while pressing downwards increases the speed of the spin. Instead of their hands held at the same height as their chest, they should be lower and more in line with a skater's belly button, because they are pressing down in the spin.

*Exiting the Spin*

Many skaters feel like they can get *into* a sit spin but getting *out* is a challenge. This is understandable, given that they are in a one-foot squat on a slick surface, while balancing on a thin piece of metal. To rise out of the spin, skaters can press down into the skating foot and use that pressure to push themselves up. Pushing up involves pressing hips forward while also squeezing glute muscles and keeping the core tight. Some skaters benefit from imagining a rope pulling them from their arms/chest and their free leg. This helps them to keep weight on the skating leg and keep the free side feeling weightless and lifting. Off-ice strength and conditioning helps skaters to develop the strength to stand out of sit spins.

Sit Spin Recap:

- Skaters sit quickly as they enter the spin
- The knee, hip, and ankle all need to bend
- The free leg should lock, turn out, and press against the skating leg - just below the kneecap
- Arms should be locked and stretched in front with hands stacked and pressing downward
- To rise out of the spin, press down into the skating foot and use that pressure to push hips forward and lift head up

*Camel Spins*

Skaters love to go into camel spins as though they are already doing a camel position from the entry edge but that position often ends up looking more like a breaching whale to me. It works so much better when skaters hold a normal entry edge, standing upright but with a bent ankle and knee, so that it looks like they are starting a scratch spin. The camel then becomes a surprise at the end of the hook and looks so much more natural and controlled.

To create the camel position, a skater locks the skating leg and sends the hips back as far as possible, while at the same time keeping the back arched. This is an important position to practice at the wall and gliding backward. It's very similar to the backward spiral position: skaters have their free leg locked, hip bent, torso facing the ice, shoulders back with an arched back, arms lifted, and chin level to the ice. I often see skaters spinning in a camel position with their chin down, facing the ice. Not only does that look like it would be nauseating on the dizzy scale, but it also affects the balance and speed of the spin. Skaters should have their chin level to the ice and eyes looking straight ahead. They should feel like the crown of the head is reaching back toward the free foot. This banana-back position increases the spin's momentum.

An important difference between spirals and camel spins is the free leg. The free leg won't lift as high as some spirals can lift (no splits in the air). Some coaches prefer a free leg that is level with the hip, and some prefer a bit higher than that. I prefer a higher free leg that is higher (closer to the height of the skater's shoulder). A higher free leg can increase the skaters' speed in the spin and helps them to keep their free hip lifted. The free hip should be stacked on top of the skating leg and the free leg should also feel as though it's pulling toward the opposite back shoulder. For example, a left foot camel spin should have the right free leg pulling toward the left shoulder – and the left shoulder should also pull toward the right free leg. Skaters should keep the free leg squeezing from the glutes to the pointed toe, throughout the entire spin.

One final piece of the camel spin that really helps skaters balance is focusing on the hips and upper body. Like the spiral drill in chapter 4, skaters hold the camel position at the wall on two feet so that they can feel how much their hips have to bend and back needs to arch. They should be able to hold something (like a glove or marker) in the bend of their hip because it is bent far enough back that it creates a little crease at the top of their leg. Skaters can master this hip bend by trying to hold something in the crease of their hip at the wall and while gliding backward. When they apply this bend to the spin and feel as though their leg is locked and torso is parallel to the ice, finding the spin spot becomes natural and eventually consistent.

Camel Spin Recap:

- ·Skaters enter a camel spin similarly to a scratch spin
- ·Skaters press their hips back as they enter a camel
- Skaters' free legs should be active through the entire camel
- Skaters should keep their heads up and back arched during a camel

# CHAPTER VII

## ICE DANCE

I love ice dance and believe it's one of the most beautiful styles of skating. The expression is gorgeous and the focus on form and edges, details and specific pattern brings my rule-following mind a lot of joy. It is the perfect combination of science and art, as the skater tests physics with deep lean and knee bend and glides across the ice with strong expression and artistry. I love coaching ice dance and have successfully coached skaters through many dance tests.

My introduction to ice dance was when I was a preteen. I decided, knowing very little about ice dance, that I wanted to become an ice dancer. Unfortunately, I only dipped my toe into ice dance and didn't continue the path in my youth. My mom found a very talented Russian coach in Colorado Springs. He was barely over 5 feet tall, wore an Elmer Fudd hat, and spoke broken English. He would take me around the ice, going through patterns while counting, and he terrified me. I have no idea why, but I was so intimidated by him, but I wish I could go back in time and tell my little preteen self to suck it up, buttercup, and learn some ice dance, because it is such an incredible part of skating.

I have revisited the world of ice dance as a coach because skaters have asked me to take them through dances. I have done as much research as I can while also applying my knowledge about moves and edges to it. One thing that I have discovered is that it is different from moves but very relatable. A lot of the things we struggle with in moves (and figures) patterns carry over into ice dance. I will share an overview about coaching dance steps and ways you can connect ice dance to moves and edges.

*Swing Rolls*

One of the things I notice most about experienced ice dancers is that their swing rolls just look *light*. I try to teach skaters to appear light in swing rolls and I think it's important for them to rise during the swing roll to create a light swing roll. Swing rolls are performed on a 4 or 6 count during a dance and a skater should begin the first half of the swing roll with the skating ankle and knee bent and then rise to pass the free leg in front (when going forward) or behind (when going backward). Skaters should feel as though it isn't just their leg that rises, but their entire body, as though a string is tied to their head, and they are being pulled upwards by the string.

I teach swing rolls with shoulders square to hips and shoulders pinched back so that a skater's back is strong, straight, and has excellent posture. A skater's chin remains level (or slightly higher than level) to the ice and eyes remain up. This is one of the many reasons that ice dance is so beneficial to skaters; it teaches excellent posture and performance skills on the ice. (The skills skaters learn about following music, rhythm, and a count are another bonus).

The free leg should be completely locked while extended, during both parts of a swing roll. During an outside swing roll, a skater will keep the free leg locked throughout the entire swing roll. During an inside swing roll, a skater bends the free leg slightly when it passes by the skating foot. Skaters should feel like there is a line drawn from their head to their free toes that stretches long to maintain the right posture. They should feel as though they are constantly pulling on this line with the crown of their head and their pointed toes. Forward swing rolls lean back quite a bit and skaters should bend a lot so that they can achieve a leaned back position.

Skaters feel like their knee, ankle, and hip lean into the lobe during swing rolls and *not* their upper bodies. Skaters sometimes tend to lean their torso into a lobe, and it causes them to break at the waist and lose their balance. It's very important that they keep their

104

head and shoulders straight on top of their hips. It should feel like a book is balanced on their head as they perform the swing rolls (this is also true for every move in ice dance).

Skaters benefit from holding a cord or exercise band, stretched across the chest or back during swing rolls, to maintain upper body awareness and keep shoulders strong and body lines long.

Swing Rolls Recap:

- Swing rolls are done on 4 and 6 counts
- Swing rolls should appear light, and skaters should bend their skating ankle and knee for the first half and straighten their ankle and knee for the second half
- Skaters should lean back during forward swing rolls and feel an imaginary line stretching from their head to their free toes
- Swing rolls lean from the lower body and not the upper body

*Chasses*

Chasses are both an elegant dance move and a useful tool for strengthening forward crossovers, deepening knee bend, and developing better extension and controlled edges.

The first push in a chasse is like the first push in a crossover (see the crossover section in chapter 4 for more details about how this push is performed). Isolating that crossover push when performing a chasse allows skaters to focus on gaining power from the push without the distraction of the second push in a crossover.

During a chasse, skaters lean into the circle the entire time. A chasse contains one push and one step, which are often repeated. The first push is like a stroke in which the outside foot rotates open, the ankle bends, and the skater pushes off the inside edge as they extend and lock their free leg, keeping it turned out. This first half of the chasse puts the skater on an outside edge on their skating leg. They should bend the skating leg and keep pressure on the outside edge the entire time.

The second portion of the chasse is when the skater lifts the inside foot slightly (only to about ankle height) and keeps it flexed. Skaters should keep their feet very close together (directly beneath their hips) during chasses. This helps skaters to maintain the proper edge. When skaters step wide, particularly from the forward inside to forward outside edge, they have a very difficult time maintaining the outside edge. The step should be close beneath the skaters' hips, and they should step their blades directly onto an outside edge. Once a skater steps onto the outside edge, they should be able to maintain a clean outside edge if they bend their ankles and stack their free hips.

Skaters can focus on strong posture, correct form, and lots of edge pressure and bends when practicing chasses.

Chasses Recap:

- Chasses begin with the first push skaters perform in a crossover
- Skaters lean into the circle throughout the whole chasse
- Skaters should extend and point on the first push of the chasse
- Skaters should step close beneath their skating hip on each step of the chasse

*Waltz Threes*

Waltz threes are a beautiful skating move when done correctly. They are performed with a six count in which skaters do the three-turn for the first three counts and the back outside edge for the second three counts. There are a few key focus points that help these to look clean, crisp, and maintain flow.

The first thing to focus on is like the other dance elements: a skater should keep the head and upper body straight and keep the shoulder blades rolled back and pulling toward one another for balance and nice posture. It can be challenging to turn and step while keeping a straight back so it's important for skaters to imagine they have something balanced on their heads or feel like a string is connected to the crown of their head and pulling them upward toward the ceiling (this is similar to upright spins).

The second thing to focus on during the waltz threes is the close step after the three-turn. A skater pulls the free leg straight, foot flexed, and keeps it beneath the free hip while turning (it helps to feel like the inner thighs are magnetic and pulling toward one another during the turn). This way, skaters can step down directly under their hips and step onto a clean back outside edge after the turn.

Skaters should be very light in their skating legs during the three-turns. They feel a soft rise and bend during the turn and the rock of the blade should look effortless because they pay close attention to the blade pressure and rock the weight of their hips forward as they rise in the skating leg. Lifting the free hip during the turn also helps the turn appear light and effortless. Skaters bend directly before and after the turn, but the actual turn occurs when the skater's leg is locked, and they rise onto the front of the blade.

The back outside edge portion of a waltz three is held on a clean edge with a lifted free hip and bent ankle. Skaters need to stretch their free legs long behind them and keep their knees locked and toes pointed, for proper extension and carriage.

Waltz threes are skated in both directions and skaters who spin counter-clockwise will do better with the left forward outside three-turn direction. The other direction will need lots of repetition. Skaters can isolate the two parts of the waltz threes to strengthen the three-turn itself and the back outside edge, without feeling rushed by keeping the timing.

Waltz Threes Recap:

- The three-turn is three counts and the back outside edge is also three counts, adding up to a total six count
- The free leg during the turn is straight and held beneath the free hip to provide a clean back outside edge step after the turn

# CHAPTER VIII

## TECHNIQUES AND DRILLS

*Hip Shift Drills*

Skaters are constantly shifting their weight between their hips on the ice, and, as they become more skilled at fully shifting their weight and shifting their weight quickly, they will have improved skating skills. Skaters shift their weight for virtually everything, for example: forward stroking, bunny hops, power pulls, crossovers, waltz jumps, alternating edges on the line, and the list could go on for pages. Therefore, practicing hip shifts is important for skaters, especially because they can confuse the feeling of lifting their *foot* as shifting their weight, and the two are different.

A simple beginning hip shift drill that is useful for Basic 1 and Adult 1 skaters is having them stand with their feet hip-width apart and bend one knee but keep the other one straight. As they do this, they should imagine their nose (their center) moving over the hip that is bent. It will not line up exactly over that hip, but they will feel a significant amount of their weight shift to that foot. They should then reverse their weight to the other knee, bending it and shift their weight again. They can do this going back and forth at a standstill and then try the drill while moving. The hip should not pop out during this drill. It should remain on top of the knee and ankle with good alignment.

Another effective hip shift drill is the penguin waddle. This drill is especially useful when learning outside edges and helping skaters to feel that their hip is lifted. Often, skaters will just lift their free knee and think that their hip is up, but there is an actual motion to lifting hips that is crucial. Isolating the knee lift helps to achieve this. A skater begins by locking legs and holding them hip width apart. Then the skater lifts one leg without bending the knee. It will require some concentration, but the result will be that the hip lifts toward the ribcage, causing the foot to dangle a few inches off the ice. The skater performs this drill on both sides and practices the drill while forward or backward moving across the ice in something like a locked leg march (the skater will resemble a penguin waddling on the ice).

After working on this drill, I usually have skaters practice holding the position they were working on (whether it's an outside edge, a stroking position, h-position, etc.) while creating the same feeling in their hip so that their hip is lifted and not just level with the other hip. The aha moment is incredible to witness. Try it, you'll see.

*Deeper Edge Drills*

Skaters tend to learn edges by following the hockey circles and performing edges that are so shallow they tend to fall flat. These shallow edges are not only difficult to perform but they are also very difficult to feel and are not true to the feeling that most edges produce when skating across the ice performing skills on edges like crossovers, cross strokes, jump take-offs, etc.

Since shallow edges are so difficult for beginner skaters, I like skaters to learn how to execute deeper edges from the start along with shallow edges. Therefore, I have skaters use the same hockey circle but hold active edges instead. Deep edges are exactly as they sound. They are edges that gain speed during the edge, tighten the lean, and deepen the knee bend as they go. Skaters can increase the angle of lean on their blade to deepen their edges.

Beginning on the hockey circle, skaters start on an outside or inside edge (this can be executed forward or backward) and, instead of following the circle, skaters bend and lean so much that

110

they take their edge toward the center dot of the circle instead. When they get good at that, skaters can try spiraling their edge (not a skating spiral – a tight circle that keeps getting smaller and smaller).

As skaters continue these deep edges, they will need to keep their skating hips tucked, continuously rotate their shoulders into the circle (because their shoulders will automatically rotate the opposite direction as they rotate on their edge) and keep constant pressure on the edge. Skaters usually enjoy edges more when they can execute a deeper edge and it allows them to gain better experience in edge control. One thing to note, if you want to change things up, skaters can also try this drill with their shoulders rotated out of the circle. They should still maintain lots of shoulder rotation pressure during the drill so that their shoulders don't end up squaring off. The counter-rotation shoulders will feel like a spin entrance.

Another edge drill is one that uses an axis and allows skaters to work on their forward and backward inside edges. Skaters can start by using one of the hockey lines as an axis and can later take the drill around the continuous axis of the rink. Standing on the axis, skaters lift their foot, open their hip, and step onto their turned open foot on an inside edge. They transfer their body weight over the inside edge foot and lift and tuck the other foot (they can imagine their belly button shifts over the new skating foot).

Skaters hold a deep, but short, inside edge from the axis and back to the axis (it creates a small arc on the ice on one side of the axis). As skaters return to the axis, they open the free foot and step onto it on the other side of the axis and continue down the line like this. It is important that skaters keep their free hip lifted and level throughout this drill. They can continuously increase the ankle bend and practice stepping onto deeper inside edges.

This drill can be executed backward down the axis as well. The difference is that skaters will rotate their hip inward to then step on their foot on an inside edge. Skaters should also

111

practice leaning back during this drill so that they can maintain pressure on the middle of the blade and keep their body from rocking too far forward to the toe pick.

Finally, this same drill can be executed as a standstill going forward or backward. The skater will continuously trace the same two lobes on either side of the axis. They can do this without moving forward or backward simply by where they step. If a skater is performing a forward inside edge on one foot, they will need to start the edge and move forward until they make it to the axis. Then, instead of stepping next to their skating foot for the next edge, they should step backwards to the spot where they had originally started their edge on the other foot and then glide forward back to where they were. They can repeat this, always stepping behind their skating foot and continuing forward so that they stay in one spot.

This same drill can be done backwards if a skater rotates their hip inward and steps on their inside edge, gliding backward toward the axis. When they reach the axis, skaters turn the free foot in and step forward, where they originally started on the other foot, shift their hip so that their weight is now over the foot they stepped on and glide backwards again. Repeat.

Edge Drills Recap:

- Deep edges are easier for skaters to feel than shallow edges
- Skaters need to continuously rotate their shoulders as they hold an edge, so that they can keep them rotated into the circle instead of getting square
- To deepen their edge, skaters can increase their ankle bend, edge pressure, and the angle of lean of their blade

*Drills for Turns*

The fascinating thing about turns is that they are all connected. Once skaters master the rock on the blade, the shoulder check, the knee bend and rise, and their edges, then they can successfully perform any turn with practice. Skaters either turn into their circle (three-turns and rockers) or the opposite direction of their circle (brackets and counters). To strengthen turning skills, drills for turns as well as lots and lots of edge practice are crucial.

There are three parts of a turn: the entry edge, the turn itself, and the exit edge. I love having skaters drill the exit edge of turns because, the more powerful their exit edges are, the more speed and flow they can create from their turns. The exit edge should feel a bit like a power pull in which skaters feel themselves pressing down into the ice, rising in their knee, and gaining speed.

One way to drill the exit edge of a turn is by having skaters perform a stop (either on one foot or two) and then lift one leg and perform a power pull in the other direction from where they were stopped. This may seem complicated when reading it, but there aren't specific rules because you can do this on any foot in any direction to work on different turns. For example, a skater can perform a one footed right hockey stop then remain on the right foot, bend their ankle, and press down and push onto a right back inside edge, rising in their knee as they go.

Skaters can do the exact same stop and push forward into a forward inside, back outside, or forward outside edge as well. The possibilities are continuous. Skaters will be challenged by starting the edge from a standstill before pressing into their blade and moving across the ice. If they gain the ability to create and maintain flow from a standstill, then they will be able to create beautiful exit edges while moving during a turn.

Another great way to practice the flow and edge quality in and out of a turn is to perform power pulls in and out of turns. For example, a skater can perform a left forward inside to outside power pull, then, as the skater changes back to the inside edge, they can rotate their shoulders into the direction of travel and perform a three-turn. The turn will end on a left back outside edge and the skater can pull out of it like a power pull then continue with power pulls by changing to the left back inside edge.

When skaters return to the back outside edge, they can rotate shoulders out of the circle and perform a back outside three-turn, ending in a forward inside edge and they can repeat. This can be done continuously down the ice and the skater could skate on the same foot all the way down the ice, repeating the power pulls and three-turns as they go.

This can be done on the other foot and can be performed with other turns. The idea behind this drill is that skaters can have crisp, strong edges and can feel themselves bending and rising throughout, like a power pull. This is an excellent skill for skaters to work on for their footwork sequences.

Turning Drills Recap:

- Skaters can perform power pulls from a stopped position to practice their exit edge of a turn
- Skaters can perform moving power pulls in between turns to practice their edges into and out of turns

*Drills for Stops*

Skaters should have a strong understanding of how their blades work and to be able to manipulate and control them on the ice in multiple ways. One of these ways that is often overlooked is stopping. Stops are important for safety, but they also have a lot to do with artistry and control.

Stops are useful in programs, especially when they go along with the music, at a place where the music stops or changes. Some skaters master spirals and spiral variations in which they skid to a stop and turn, and it is a very elegant move on the ice. Despite all of this, I find it surprising that there are so many skaters, even at high levels, who cannot stop on both feet, or one footed, and in all directions. These skills demonstrate mastery of the blade and strong control, and skaters should work on being able to manipulate their blades to skid across the ice in all directions, not just the ones that are strong for them.

A drill that I particularly like, which helps with stops on both sides, is when skaters perform standstill skid-stops, sliding back and forth but remaining in one spot on the ice. Skaters begin with feet hip-width apart, toes pointed forward, in line with knees and hips, then they lift their right foot, step onto it, and slide their weight to the right, with weight evenly distributed throughout the blade and on a *very slight* inside edge (if skaters lean toward an outside edge, they will often get their blade stuck into the ice, unable to move).

During this drill, the skaters' ankles should remain bent, and they should have weight pressing down into the ice. They should shift their weight over their skating foot as they slide to the right. Next, they set down the left foot and shift their weight, pushing off the right foot as they step onto the left, sliding over their stopping spot to the left. Skaters draw a skid mark across the ice on the right and then the left, basically performing a stopping motion while standing on one foot and switching from one side to the other. The skater's body remains facing the same direction the entire time. This drill continues back and forth, standing in one place. It can be very difficult for some skaters to master but it is very helpful with stopping, skidding, and blade mastery.

*Stops that Start with a Turn*

One thing that can easily go unnoticed in skating is that a lot of the stops we do begin with a turn. They aren't necessarily a full 180 degree turn like a three-turn or bracket, but they are done the same form and turn 90 degrees instead.

Hockey stops are examples of these 90 degrees turns. Skaters begin with the standard *bend, rise, bend* method, and rotate their hips 90 degrees in one direction while they turn their shoulders the other direction during the rise. During the rise, skaters will rock to the front of their blade and rotate the hips one direction, shoulders the other direction. Immediately after the rise, skaters will bend and press into their arch. Rather than glide on an edge like a skater would do during a three-turn, the skater is going to lean back and press into their skid spot on the blade. (That lean on a hockey stop would result in the foot that is further forward being on an inside edge and the back foot leaning onto an outside edge).

Skaters can take these hockey stops and transform them into any turns they want by rocking on their blade and rotating in different directions. Hockey stops can be performed on one foot on the forward inside edge foot by lifting the back foot or on the outside edge foot by lifting the front foot and turning on the back foot only (this puts skaters on an outside edge and is slightly more difficult).

To improve at this one footed stop, skaters can practice doing a regular hockey stop and lifting one foot at the very end of the stop to get used to the balance and lean on that foot. Once they are comfortable with the one foot at the end of the stop, they can practice the full turn and stop on one foot. This can also include gliding backward and turning to stop by rocking to the heel.

Skaters can use these choreographic stops in step sequences or throughout programs to add an interesting dynamic or dramatic moment. However, regardless of how they are used, it's a great mark of skating ability to be able to turn and stop in each direction on each foot.

# CHAPTER IX

# GROUP INSTRUCTION

Group classes are often associated with different challenges than private instruction. Some of these challenges include balancing skaters at different abilities, skater conflict/disrespect, safety in managing large numbers of skaters, keeping everyone interested/engaged, and instructing different learning styles. When working with large groups of people, there are always unexpected bumps along the way, but having a plan helps, so I will share some tips that have worked for me when encountering these challenges.

*Keeping Group Lessons Fun*

Group lessons need to be fun- not just for the skaters - but for the coach as well. I think there is a stigma that coaching group classes is boring, especially when it's a basic skills class, but I'd like to challenge coaches to break that stigma and find ways to enjoy group classes. I used to think they were boring too. Somehow, a thirty-minute group lesson could drag on for what felt like longer than two hours of private lessons. But then I realized that there are more skaters involved in the group lessons and there are ways to make it interesting.

I remember one day I was teaching a Basic 2 class and I was thinking about how coaching my private lesson Basic 2 skater was so much more fun because we were working on choreography for her competition program. Then it occurred to me that these skaters could also work on choreography, and it may even help them to enjoy skating more. So, for the last five minutes of class, we made up a program together.

We started with a simple beginning pose and then counted out some elements they were working on, such as two-foot turns and backward swizzles. We added graceful arm movements to these elements, and it made practicing them more fun for the skaters. I even added elements that weren't in any level but are beneficial to learn, like marching in a circle and walking on toe picks. We ended with a pose and practiced curtsying on the ice. The skaters in my class loved it and I felt the time going by more quickly because we were all involved in something interesting and having fun.

There are lots of games that we play off the ice that can also be played on the ice. Tag is not one of my favorites because it seems like someone gets injured each time it's played - not to mention that, at my rink, we catch young skaters playing tag on freestyle ice all the time and I generally prefer not to encourage it. One game that I love playing with Snowplow and Basic 1 skaters is Simon Says. This is a fun game on the ice because you can get creative and have skaters do more than just the elements that are in their level. I like to have them try things that get them more comfortable with the ice, such as touching the ice, touching their toes (because it encourages bending) and having a dance party so that they can be silly and express themselves on the ice.

A few other ideas are creating obstacle courses, singing songs with skaters like; "Going on a Bear Hunt" and having them follow you along on the hunt, and "Head, Shoulders, Knees, and Toes" (I love that song because skaters it gets skaters to bend as they touch their knees and toes).

Blasting off into space is a fun game as well. To play this game, skaters count down from ten (young skaters love this) and push themselves off the wall to either practice backward wiggles or backward swizzles. Usually, when we "land" on the moon, I have skaters pretend they are skating around without gravity, and they have a lot of fun with that. Trust me, these games keep skaters engaged but they also make it much more fun for the coaches, so it's a win-win.

*Safety in Managing Large Numbers of Skaters*

The day will come when you encounter that overwhelming group of skaters that feel like an unsafe situation, and you may want to run off the ice and never look back. I know I've been there and it's usually from a beginner class like Basic 1, Adult 1, or Snowplow Sam 1. New skaters, particularly young skaters, don't understand the danger that their skates represent to other skaters. They also don't understand that they are human dominoes when they stand near each other on the ice.

I think these classes work best when they begin off the ice, teaching skaters how to march, safely fall, and get up before they even set foot on the ice. (This is also a great time to check that skates fit properly and are laced correctly). Once skaters step on the ice, I usually spend a large portion of the first class keeping them spread apart. During a hectic class when they are all falling into each other, I have been known to sit them all down and just talk while sitting then spread skaters out before having them stand one at a time. It's a cold experience, but they have to learn that skating is cold sometime, right? Plus, it's a good thing that beginner group classes are usually just thirty minutes.

During the first lesson, I also show skaters how to balance themselves -and basically freeze and stand still on the ice- when they feel like they are falling backwards. They can do this by bending their knees and touching their knees with their hands. It's basically a way to keep skaters from locking their legs and leaning back onto their heels. I've seen this work well for skaters who continuously fall backwards and it's a useful tool for when a new skater has someone fall near them. I tell them to freeze and touch their knees until the other skater stands up again (my biggest fear is creating a football field pileup on the ice with skates flying every which way in a beginner group lesson). This position helps them to stand still and not slide forward or backward on their skates.

*Instructing Different Learning Styles*

During my years as a teacher, I observed that everyone learns differently, and you can't expect the same outcome from everyone if you present information in the exact same way. Some people are auditory learners, some are visual, and some are kinesthetic, although I like to think that most people are a mix of all of these, to some degree. When presenting something on the ice, I try to visually represent to the skaters some form of what I'm teaching (don't worry, you don't have to demonstrate a double lutz for a skater to teach it- if you're like me, you've had enough injuries by the time you're an adult skater that demonstrating jumps isn't probable). I demonstrate the arm positions, walk-through the jumps, show skaters the edge, etc. Even on the days that my body hurts and won't allow me on the ice, I still find myself demonstrating from the boards as I teach.

While showing the element, I also talk it out, describing the detailed steps and the feeling of what they are trying to achieve so that they understand. Additionally, I have the skaters walk through it slowly with me or hold positions on the wall so that they can feel it as well and learn kinesthetically. You may discover in private lessons which skaters you can simply explain things to, and which need to be shown or need to walk through it more often, but in a group setting, it's very helpful to use all three forms of learning. I also don't think it hurts for skaters to be taught things all three ways, even if they respond better to one way. It helps those skaters to develop a greater understanding of technique.

*Variations*

Offering variations of things in a group setting is also beneficial for the class. If you've ever taken a yoga class where the teacher does a headstand but allows you to remain safely in child's pose, you probably have a strong appreciation of variations. A few examples of providing variations are; having more advanced skaters work on crossovers while others practice pumps on the circle, allowing more advanced skaters to do cross strokes down the length of the ice, while others practice maintaining deep edges in slaloms, or have some skaters practice two foot spins, while more advanced skaters work on different positions like camel, sit, scratch, or flying spins.

Providing variations gives skaters an idea of where they are heading while also keeping the group working on similar patterns across the ice. Skaters can see that if they work hard on their single jumps and landing positions that they will progress to the more advanced jumps in the future while they learn from seeing other skaters practice them.

One final thought: don't forget to learn from skaters as well. Pay close attention to their "aha moments" and how they describe what they are doing. It's easy for us to get lost in the professional dialogue revolving around the sport and to forget that sometimes saying it simply is what's best. I was recently coaching an adult skater on swizzles and tried several different ways to explain to her that she needed to bend her knees. Finally, I had her try rocking horses slowly and she started bending with each push. She had a moment where she looked at me and said, "Oh, I see, I have to *lower* myself toward the ice *a lot.*" I was so excited that she had started to bend and understood how it felt. I made a mental note to tell her in future lessons to "lower herself to the ice" rather than "bend."

There have been times where I have said something in different ways only for a skater to stop and exclaim, "Oh I get it now!" after the tenth way of saying the exact same thing. The good news is that there are *a lot* of correct ways to teach things and open mindedness opens the door to progress.

*Keeping the Group Engaged*

The way you go about keeping a group of skaters involved and excited about class is going to vary depending on what type of class you are instructing. The first thing to consider is what the goal is for the class, based on the class you are teaching. A first day Snowplow Sam class may simply need the goal of the skaters getting comfortable with the ice and getting to know the coach, while a Power class will have goals of helping skaters increase stamina and endurance and making sure they are worn out by the time the class is over.

Sometimes the goals will be apparent, like in the two classes mentioned above, and sometimes you may have to find out more information to understand the goals you need to meet. For example, a Basic 4 class has written goals which are the required elements that the skaters must learn and work toward mastering. However, it helps to get to know the skaters in the class because some skaters may be working on their Basic 4 edges for speed skating, hockey, or figure skating and some may simply be taking the class to get some exercise and because it's fun.

I find it helps to know where the skaters are coming from so that you can support their goals by making the work they are doing relatable in the long run. If a skater is planning to skate on a hockey team, it can be helpful to not just talk about edges in the sense of being used for jumps and spin entries, but to explain how skaters need to be quick and have proper edge control to skate well during a game.

Another important thing to note when dealing with a group is to always have a back-up plan. For example, in a Jump's class, you may have a detailed plan ready for axel prep only to discover that none of the skaters in the class have started working on axels. It's helpful to bring all the skaters together at the beginning of the class to find out what level they are and what their goals are, and then make sure the class structure can meet some or all of their needs.

Things can get tricky, but not impossible, when working with several different levels at one time. There are certain things that skaters working on ½ jumps, singles, doubles, and triples have in common, including landing positions, air positions, and take-off edges. Skaters can work on those as a group even if the positions will be applied to different jumps. More advanced skaters can also demonstrate elements to other skaters which can be a great motivational tool for skaters who are looking to advance.

Group Skating Recap:

- Always discuss safety and personal space on the ice and teach skaters to freeze and watch out for other skaters who have fallen
- People learn differently so be prepared to teach to many different learning styles and include kinesthetic, visual, and auditory teaching styles in a group setting
- Be creative and have fun
- Be sure to know the goals of each class so that you can have a clear direction in each class
- Prepare for classes so that skaters can be challenged enough at their level in classes

# CHAPTER X

## OFF - ICE STRENGTH AND CONDITIONING

Skaters exercise each time they skate on the ice so there are often questions about why they should do strength and conditioning off the ice as well. This is something of a pet-peeve of mine and I could rant about it for a while, so I will try to keep my description concise. Off-ice strength and conditioning has everything to do with a skater's success and safety. Figure skating is difficult and requires strength and stamina, both of which needs to be developed off of the ice. Skating without conditioning is also dangerous. Skaters need strong and limber muscles in order to perform the elements on the ice that are expected of them.

*Stretches are Not Warm-ups, Young Lady*

Okay, yes, that was told to me once. I knew that warming up was the process of getting the muscles moving so that you could then workout and stretch with less chance of injury, but I froze during a PSA ratings exam when asked what a warm-up was and part of my answer included "stretching." I was reamed. Moral of the story, stretches are *not* a part of skaters' warm-ups. However, skaters should still stretch *after* warming up and before getting onto the ice.

It's really up to each coach as to what they prefer skaters to use as warm-ups, but they are a great habit to form early on in skating. Some examples of exercises that I have had skaters use as warm-ups include; jump roping (or invisible jump roping), high knees, jogging, quick squats, squat jumps, grapevines, and forward and backward skipping (backward skipping is great for coordination).

A realistic goal for new skaters would be to arrive 15-20 minutes before the skating session starts and plan for five to ten minutes of light cardio to warm up and five minutes of stretching. However, it is up to each coach to decide how much time they feel is adequate for a warm-up. The important thing is that skaters are consistent about warming up and make sure that they are moving enough that their muscles are warm before they stretch or get on the ice. The self-discipline that skaters learn in developing these types of healthy habits become lifelong skills for them.

Warm-Ups Recap:

- Skaters should get their muscles moving with light cardio before stretching, working out, or getting on the ice
- Developing a daily warm-up routine develops lifelong habits for skaters

*Developing Strength and Conditioning Plans*

Strength and conditioning could be an entire book. Each coach will have their own ideas about what they'd like skaters to work on in strength and conditioning. I am going to give a brief overview as well as some sample workouts that coaches could use for strength and conditioning.

Strength and conditioning should always begin with a warm-up and end with a cool down. Coaches can choose to give skaters workouts that focus each day on a different part of the body or to have skaters participate in a full body workout. If I am working with skaters for a week in a skating camp, I will usually break it down day by day into something like this:

Day One: Lower Body

Warm up with a light jog. Skaters perform a circuit of walking lunges, squats, and wall sits. I always like to include something that keeps skaters' heart rates up during a circuit, such as squats, jump rope, or squat jumps. Skaters can work other leg muscles in the next circuit with heel raises, step ups, and side leg lifts. Skaters cool down with a side shuffle, skipping, and slow jump roping. It's helpful to do light cardio after a workout to help prevent lactic acid build up. Skaters should finish by stretching their legs and hold their stretches at least thirty seconds while deepening their stretches each time they exhale so that their muscles are relaxed.

Day Two: Upper Body

Warm up by jogging stairs. Skaters perform a circuit of push-ups, slow arm circles (hold arms straight out and rotate in small circles forward and then backward), and bench presses. Next skaters can use weights to do bicep curls, lateral raises, and tricep extensions. Skaters can cool down with forward and backward skips and a brisk walk. Skaters should stretch their upper body muscles.

Day Three: Core

Skaters can warm up with burpees (everyone's favorite exercise), high knees, and jumping jacks. The circuit can consist of holding a plank, supermans, and v-ups. Next, skaters can do a circuit of leg lifts (lift legs and lower slowly while lying on back), side planks, and sit ups (I usually choose sit ups instead of crunches since people often just pull on their necks during crunches instead of working out their core muscles). Skaters can cool down with cross jacks (jump and cross feet then uncross them), butt kicks, and toy soldiers (these are walking, controlled stretches).

These were all examples of brief exercises to get coaches and skaters started. The main idea is to include a warm-up and cool down and provide a variety of different exercises for skaters. I encourage you to expand on them and put your own creativity into the circuits.

Conditioning Plans Recap:

- Be sure that skaters warm-up and cool down during workouts
- You can create circuits that focus on one area of the body but work the muscles differently

*Using Games for Off-Ice Conditioning*

Let's face it, not all skaters are going to enjoy off-ice, but it is so important to skating that they still need to give their best effort. Some of the times that I have seen skaters put in the most effort in off-ice strength and conditioning have been when they are playing games that center around exercises.

Sharks and minnows and freeze tag are two games that will get skaters running as fast as they can to help them develop stamina. Pretty much tag in any form excites them and takes the focus off the fact that they are doing a lot of cardio. There are so many variations out there, such as color tag, blob tag (if they are tagged, they join hands and run as a blob to tag the others), and crabwalk or bear crawl tag (they chase each other while crab walking/bear crawling).

Another tried and true method for off-ice that keeps skaters motivated are relays. I have seen a lot of creative relays over the years. Coaches can add props that skaters have to pick up and bring to a certain spot, while racing the other group. They can challenge coordination with three-legged races or wheelbarrow races and can keep skaters moving with a variety of exercises like walking spiral positions or h-position skipping.

Obstacle courses are another good way to keep workouts interesting. During these, skaters can go through a series of exercises while racing their time. Here's an example of an obstacle course: hula hoop/jump rope a certain number of times, run up and down a staircase, do lunges to the other end of the room, pick up weights and do squats with them, bear crawl to another part of the room, hold a plank, and then end with an off-ice axel or waltz jump. There are so many possibilities of exercises to do even if you don't have a lot of workout equipment. Marking spots on the floor with guards or tape can work wonders.

Sometimes, just making the workout into a competition changes everything. Figure skaters are competitive, so it plays off their strengths right away. I've had skaters compete on how long they can hold wall sits and suddenly skaters who complained over a one-minute wall sit can hold them for ten minutes (it's amazing how that happens). Skaters can also compete with planks, boat pose (feet and arms in the air, balancing on backside and using core), and standing and balancing on one leg (after about a minute, this becomes a workout). To make wall sit competitions more interesting, sometimes I have skaters play hot potato during it. This is where they are lined up against the wall and pass something back and forth while music plays. If the music stops, the skater holding the object has to do some agreed upon challenge.

I love partnering skaters up during an off-ice conditioning class. Not only is it more fun to work together, but it keeps skaters motivated since they are working with another skater directly, rather than just being an individual part of a group. There are lots of ways to create partner exercises. One way is to pair skaters up in a circuit and give each pair two exercises (for example, one does a wall sit while the other holds a plank. They can switch between the two exercises in an assigned amount of time.

Additionally, any exercise in which skaters can high five during reps is always a hit. Here are a few examples: they can face one another during a high plank and keep switching hands from one to the other as they high five one another. It's difficult to hold a plank on one arm but they won't want to leave their partner hanging so it's a great way to keep them moving. Skaters can high five in between squats, burpees, push-ups, and so much more. Never underestimate the power of a high five to keep kids going.

128

Games Recap:

- Young skaters will often work harder when they are focusing on fun games and competing
- Some useful games are variations of tag, relay races, and creative obstacle courses
- Skaters can compete with one another in wall sits, sit ups, push-ups, planks, races, etc.

*Off-Ice Jumps*

Off-ice jumps, when performed correctly, are incredibly beneficial to skaters. Coaches all have different opinions on off-ice jumps. Some avoid them because of the risk of injuries, while some won't teach a jump on ice until it is mastered off the ice. It's up to each individual coach, but I believe there are safe and effective ways to practice off-ice jumps so that skaters can improve their jump performance on the ice.

The important thing to remember when jumping off the ice is that skaters have a lot less ankle support in their shoes than in their boots. Skaters should practice jumps in properly fitted tennis shoes that have arch support. They should jump on flooring that is absorbent (ice rink lobby floors are great for this).

Skaters also need to be mindful to not perform three-turn motions on the floor like they do on the ice. On the ice, there is very little friction and a skater's entire leg rotates as one when they turn, but, off the ice, skaters could try to turn their knee or ankle and their foot will remain planted. This motion can result in serious injuries in skaters' joints. Instead, skaters should hop while they turn so that their entire leg, from the hip to the ball of the foot, rotates together.

Off-ice jumps should focus on control, quick rotation, and air position. There are lots of drills skaters can practice off-ice for jumps. Skaters can hold their landing position on each leg and slowly hop and rotate their hips while hopping in a slow and controlled circle. The goal of this exercise is to maintain proper alignment and good form as they hop, so that each time they land, they are still aligned. Their knee, ankle, and hip should be lined up and their shoulders checked with their head rotated over the skating side.

There is a similar drill for the h-position, in which skaters hop in small circles in an h-position. They should keep their free hip up and rotated inward and their shoulders checked against their hips the entire time. Skaters can even go from their h-position to their d-position while hopping in a slow and controlled circle. The d-position is the position skaters will enter when they practice axels or double jumps. In this position, their elbows will squeeze close to their upper body and their ankles will be locked together with the free hip still lifted.

Quarter turns, half turns, and full turns are a great way for skaters to work on their control, height, rotation, and alignment. Skaters start by making sure that their knees, ankles and hips are lined up. Next, skaters bend to load the muscles and then spring off their ankles and lock their legs to lift into the air. As they lift, they rotate their bodies so that their shoulders remain checked, and their hips turn beneath them. For example, a skater can start the jump with shoulders square over their hips and then rotate their hips a quarter turn under them while in the air so that the skater lands with the shoulders checked over one hip (the right hip if jumping counterclockwise). Skaters can repeat this with half turns and full turns as well.

Skaters can repeat this drill going both directions (their jump direction as well as the other way). They can even practice quickness by jumping one direction then quickly jumping and rotating the other direction. When switching directions, skaters should remember to switch their shoulders.

Skaters can perform any of their on-ice jumps if they hop during their three-turn and do small hops to replace the curve of the entry edge as they begin any jump. When a skater lands, they should also allow themselves to hop in a slow circle if needed, to take away any chance of a skater stopping one joint moving while the others continue, since this could result in an injury. Performing the jumps off ice is a great way to increase height and rotation.

Off-Ice Jumps Recap:

- Skaters can suffer injuries if they don't jump in the right shoes or on the right surfaces
- Skaters shouldn't perform three-turn motions off ice during jumps
- Skaters can use off ice jumps practice to work on proper form and alignment

# CHAPTER XI

## ADULT SKATING

I wanted to dedicate an entire chapter to adult skating for several reasons. One, adults learn differently than children and coaches should understand this and be able to adapt their coaching strategies to meet the needs of skaters of all ages. Two, the benefits and experience of coaching adults is different than coaching children and I thought I'd share some of my personal experiences as both a child skater and an adult skater and my experiences with coaching both age groups. Three, I strongly believe that adult skating is incredible, and I hope that the numbers of adult skaters will continuously grow in this world.

I think there are coaches out there who are consistently looking for the newest, youngest skaters so that they can teach them all they know as a blank slate, but I'd like to challenge that outlook and describe why choosing to also coach adult skaters would be one of the best decisions you ever make as a coach.

*Coaching Adults is Awesome*

Picture a long morning of lessons that begins at 5:30. You run out of hot coffee by 6:00. Your feet are dying by 7:00. By 7:30, your body is entering the beginning stages of hypothermia and you are beginning to doubt all your life decisions that led you to choose an ice sport. Then, 8:00 rolls around, all the kids have gone to school, and you have your lesson with your adult skater. All pretenses gone, you can talk to this adult skater, who also probably has aches and pains, who also understands that one coffee was not enough this morning, and who probably is just as annoyed at whatever happenings are taking place at the rink as you are (because

132

there is always something).   It is so refreshing to be able to speak candidly during a lesson or share an eye roll moment together.

A coach is always more than just a coach: coaches are mentors and, I believe this is especially true when coaching adults. Often, coaches are adult skaters too. They can relate to the adults they coach, and they have the opportunity to inspire adult skaters to overcome fear and setbacks as they meet them in skating. I absolutely love it. Some of the lessons that I look forward to the most each week are the lessons that I have with adult skaters.

I laugh more in adult lessons.  Generally, adult skaters put less pressure on themselves and look at their sport with humor which makes lessons interesting and light-hearted.  Coaches and skaters of all ages alike have the most random falls at times, but I find that the adult skaters tend to have the most fun laughing at the random falls and seeing things in a comical view.  In my experience, adult skaters are more likely to make hilarious comments about difficult moves, let you know when a position you are trying to have them achieve on the ice is "sorcery," and include sound effects, commentary, and other entertainment when meeting the struggles of a new skill.

Also, it's a great thing, to not have to stop a lesson because a skater is cold, wants to know how the ice stays frozen, decides to make a snowball, or licks the ice.  We've all been there.  And there's a time and a place for those fun lessons with kids.  But let's take a minute to hear it for the adults who don't care how the ice stays frozen, just that it does, and who have witnessed too many hockey games and power classes to have any urge to lick the ice, no matter how thirsty they may be.  Adult lessons are amazing.

*Helping Adults to Master New Skills*

I want to reiterate that, while the process of coaching adults can be fun, it is also very goal driven.  Helping adults to reach their goals is a great experience because adults have self-discipline and the drive to work toward goals.   Adult skaters often have more

133

obstacles to overcome than children do (one of the most common obstacles is often having less time and energy to devote to skating than children have) and their joy when they master a skill is contagious. I find myself yelling and jumping around whenever an adult correctly performs a skill that they've been working toward simply because I know how much work was put into it for the adult and how excited they will be.

Adults progress at a different pace than children and teens. They usually have less free time to skate, and they sometimes have less agility with falls, recovery, etc. However, the self-discipline is usually there and the concentration to really master a certain skill is incredibly helpful.

When an adult, who understands work ethic and takes the time to prioritize meaningful practice on and off the ice, takes the time to work toward a goal, it's amazing to see the results. I once coached an adult skater who took more skating tests in a year (for several different tracks) than any skater I had ever worked with. She was able to narrow down her goals, focus on the tasks at hand, and utilize her ice time to the best of her ability.

Sometimes adults face fear on the ice. Children do too, but it's more common in adults. One obvious reason is that adults understand what could go wrong and have experienced more injuries in their lives. Children tend to feel invincible, while adults recognize risks. I love witnessing adults work through their fear and push themselves past their comfort zones. Not only does it help them in their skating abilities, it is also a growth experience for the skater and coach.

*Adults vs. Children*

Adults and children learn differently. The things I have witnessed and discovered will not be true across the board for all people in each age group, since everyone is unique, but I think it's a helpful start to have a better understanding of how adults perceive things on the ice vs. how children perceive things.

Children and teens tend to skate more by feeling and watching, while adults analyze, want to understand the mechanics, and sometimes overthink things. The ways I explain things to children versus adults are often very different because of these differences. There are times I hold back on what I share with an adult who tends to overthink how something is done. Instead of technical details, I prefer to summarize how the element feels.

At other times, it's really satisfying to explain something to an adult who pays close attention to the corrections that need to be made and recognizes how to correct them. As an adult who learns in a similar fashion, it's easy to relate to a similar way of thinking and explain things so that they make sense.

Adults may be more analytical, while children may be more likely to see something and copy it. Skaters, who begin as children, tend to skate more by feeling, while adults will skate more by thinking. My goal for adult skaters is to teach them the proper positioning and pressure of certain edges, turns, jumps, etc. so that they can get used to doing them correctly automatically and transition from thinking about the element to feeling the element.

One amazing thing to note about adult skaters is they can make excellent coaches since they remember what it *feels like* to learn certain moves on the ice. Coaches who started skating as children may need to try to do things the opposite direction from the way we skate (for example, try a right foot waltz jump if you usually take off on the left foot). This way, we can feel how awkward and challenging skating elements are and relate better to the skaters we coach. But adult skaters can relate well to the feeling of things being new and can provide useful tips to learn new skills.

Adult skating is something that I hope continues to grow. Many rinks provide adult skating classes, sessions, and events.  It's great to foster the adult skating community and keep figure skating a sport that is open to people of all ages.  There are so many adults out there who wish they'd learned to skate, and I hope that they recognize it's never too late.

# CHAPTER XII

## DEVELOPING A COACHING PHILOSOPHY

When people lack goals, ambition, and a firm understanding of their values, they begin to travel in circles, not progressing forward, or worse, they get pulled in directions that are wrong for them. As a coach, there are many ways that you can approach the job and there will be countless people trying to tell you what to believe, how to behave, and how you should coach. Developing a coaching philosophy that fits your beliefs is critical to remain grounded in who you are as a coach. Your philosophy can guide you in your daily decision making and practices.

The process of developing your coaching philosophy will be ever changing as you grow and encounter new situations and discover new things about yourself and your skating community. Your coaching philosophy should stem from your core values so that it truly aligns with who you are, and you can remain authentic as a coach. Your experiences as a skater and as a coach along with your other roles in this world can have a positive impact on your philosophy.

The core values that I choose to follow are ones that I see in people that I respect and look up to. After all, our values should be centered around being people that we like and can be proud of. I prefer people who act out of integrity, take responsibility for their actions, and can speak honestly about what they believe in while remaining respectful to others who may disagree with them. I do my best each day to make decisions based on those values and to center myself around people who share the same values as me. A person who will change their belief system based on who they are talking

137

to loses my trust. I also do my best to maintain space from people who cannot be respectful toward others with differing opinions.

Your values may be different from mine and your life experiences will lead you to know what they are as you develop your coaching philosophy.

**Step 1:** Make a list of your core values based off your life experiences and belief systems

*Know your Goals*

To know what your philosophy is, you need to know which direction you are headed. For example, I value being a recreational coach. There are many coaches out there who would like to take skaters to world competitions and work with the most competitive skaters in the country. While I respect that and love that there are coaches willing to take on that role, I know that it isn't the lifestyle for me. It's important to look inward and decide where you see yourself as a coach, what your strengths are, and what type of coaching environment you prefer.

After years of coaching, I've learned that I enjoy working with athletes who work hard to achieve their realistic goals and I love supporting skaters in their pursuits of testing, performing, competing, and progressing in the sport. I know how much joy skating can bring to people's lives and I like to help skaters to see the rink as a place to grow, laugh, form friendships, and overcome obstacles. I enjoy seeing skaters challenge themselves, learn from setbacks, and practice good sportsmanship.

I believe coaches should be authentic, honest, and willing to speak openly to their coworkers and the skating community when conflicts arise. I strive to be a positive influence, mentor, guide, and support person for the skaters I work with. I think it can be very easy to get pulled into the competitive skating world and forget that the most important thing we can do as coaches is to have a positive impact on skaters' lives.

**Step 2:** Make a list of your goals as a coach. Think about the type of coaching environment you prefer and the type of people you would like to surround yourself with every day.

*Know Who You Are Not*

Sometimes, at competitions, I see coaches yelling at young skaters, pushing other coaches out of the way so that they can get close to the ice and throwing their arms in the air because their Basic 3 skater is going too slowly during their warm-up. (I'm not making this up). Early in my career, I decided that a certain form of coaching was not for me. I prefer to be the coach who stands quietly by the wall, chatting with skaters when they need me and reminding them to do their best. I don't need to put on the show and the skaters don't need the pressure. While we learn a lot from others about the person we want to be, we can also learn who we don't want to be and that can be equally beneficial. Everyone we encounter in figure skating has something important to teach us. To be honest, a lot of the time the lessons are in what *not* to do. But I'll take all the lessons I can get.

In addition to learning from others, I also learned from myself who I was not going to be. There have been times that I have been overly competitive and have acted conceited as a coach and skater. The regret I feel from those times has taught me to work towards humbling myself in the future. There have also been experiences where I didn't speak up against a statement or behavior and I know I should have. I once coached a skater who would become hysterical if she didn't place well in a competition even though the placement was due to a lack of practice. I am ashamed to say that I was too afraid of her family's reaction to teach her better sportsmanship and to increase her work ethic since she was disappointed with her results. I lost that teaching moment out of

139

fear about speaking up. That experience taught me to say what I believe even during times when I know it is not what someone wants to hear.

People sometimes don't want to hear the truth and there have been a lot of times where this has been a struggle for me. I once had a parent try to pressure me into allowing her daughter to test when I knew her daughter wasn't ready. It has always been one of my beliefs that a skater should present a strong test to the judges and have a certain level of edge control and power before progressing to the next level. I am not a fan of shortcuts in life *or* in skating. I told this parent that I like for skaters to build a strong foundation as they progress, rather than rushing through the process only to find gaps in their skating when they arrive at the next level. This decision did not work for the parent, and she chose to fire me, twist my words, and spread rumors at the rink that I said her daughter was a terrible skater.

While these rumors were difficult for me to hear, I was able to continue doing my job and remain strong because I knew that I had acted professionally and avoided a behavior that I chose not to stand for: I wasn't going to be the coach who rushed skaters through levels when they weren't ready or who folded to every demand made by a parent or skater just to please them. Knowing my belief system as well as what I *disagree with* has helped me to make mature decisions and stick to them. It's not always easy and there are often times when people get upset, but it's important to remember the ways in which I will not behave and the choices I won't make.

Over time as a coach, you will discover more behaviors you don't want to follow. It's important to pay attention and note who you want to be and who you don't want to be.

**Step 3:** Make a list of behaviors you *won't* stand for and know the kind of coach that you choose *not* to be

140

*Be Transparent*

It is so important for skaters and their families to know your mission, values, and coaching philosophy so that they know what they can and cannot expect from you. Each time I begin lessons with a new skater, I send my lesson policy to them with a copy of my mission statement enclosed:

> My mission is to provide a safe, fun, and encouraging environment, instilling a love for figure skating while being a positive role model in athletes' lives. I strive to meet the needs of each athlete based on their individual skating level and specific goals as an athlete.

Not everyone agrees with my mission and that's okay. I have had skaters switch coaches because I stayed true to my beliefs, and it didn't fit their goals. Losing a skater can be discouraging but I just remind myself that the beauty in life is that we are all different and, if I try to morph into someone who pleases everyone, then I will risk losing myself along the way (cliche, I know, but so true)! Standing firm in your values can be very difficult, especially when others are angry with you for not changing for them, but I think authenticity is far greater than people-pleasing. Although people may generally like a people pleaser, they will have more respect for someone who remains consistent, honest, and authentic in their beliefs.

**Step 4:** Make sure others know your philosophy and remain transparent

*Don't be Afraid to Learn from Others*

I struggle with perfectionism and self-blame when something I do isn't perfect. I realize this is ridiculous since no one is perfect and I have countless faults as a human. However, I have a difficult time accepting mistakes that I make. This has affected how willing I am to learn from others because, when another coach gives me feedback on something that I missed, I go down the road of self-blame with the "how could I have missed that?" thoughts

141

trailing along with me. It's a dangerous road to travel and I don't recommend it. However, if you find yourself there, remember that, just as the skaters we work with are unique and have different perspectives, so are coaches. It's okay to not be perfect. I'm going to repeat that since my audience are mostly figure skaters and we tend to forget that fact frequently: *It's okay to not be perfect.*

Through my journey against perfectionism, I have been able to team up with some incredible coaches and learn from them. There are times when this is difficult for me because I have to remind myself when another coach shows me a better technique or way of explaining something that it's okay that I wasn't teaching it as well before. Each day is an opportunity to start new and continue enhancing our skills. Life is about growth, and we are constantly learning and improving, otherwise we would find ourselves stagnant and life would become dull. As coaches, I think a growth mindset is a healthy mindset. One of the best ways to grow is by learning from others and humbling ourselves enough to know that we don't have all the answers.

**Step 5:** Grow and change over time and allow your philosophy to grow with you

*Find your Strengths*

I never enjoyed coaching so much as when I teamed up with another coach at our rink who was the yin to my yang when it came to figure skating. We both had different areas of coaching that we preferred and different perspectives to bring to skaters, but we shared the same belief systems and goals as coaches. I had so much respect for her values that she helped me to strengthen my philosophy and grow as a coach as well as an individual. I highly recommend finding other coaches that you trust and respect to team up with. Not only will it benefit your skaters, but the possibilities for learning from other coaches and having a support system are incredible.

As a team coach, I was able to fully focus on the areas of skating that were my strengths, while having full confidence that my team coach was working with skaters in other areas. We were able to reference one another with questions and support one another when conflicts with skating families arose. Having a team and a support system made a huge difference for me as a coach as well as for the skaters I coach because I was able to fully focus on the areas in skating where I excel as a coach and the skaters got the best from both of us.

**Step 6:** Recognize the areas where you are amazing and build on those

# Acknowledgements

Thank you to my parents for the early mornings, skates, freestyle sessions, and lessons. Your dedication to my dream is what got me here.

Thank you, Michael, for supporting me through the late-night writing sessions and always being there for me. Thank you, Jake, for being my little muse.

Thank you, Jolyn, for being there every step of the way. Your ability to see the bigger picture to ideas and challenges never ceases to amaze me. Thanks for pulling me over all the roadblocks to help me reach the finish line.

Thank you, Katie, for your creativity and enthusiasm and Jason, for always believing in me.